SHALLOW DISCOURSE PARSING FOR GERMAN

Dissertations in Artificial Intelligence

Artificial Intelligence (AI) is one of the fastest growing research areas in computer science with a strong impact on various fields of science, industry, and society. This series publishes excellent doctoral dissertations in all sub-fields of AI, ranging from foundational work on AI methods and theories to application-oriented theses.

Editor-in-Chief:
Professor Dr. Ralph Bergmann
Department of Business Information Systems II, University of Trier,
54286 Trier, Germany

Volume 351

Previously published in this series:

ISSN 0941-5769 (print)
ISSN 2666-2175 (online)

Shallow Discourse Parsing for German

Peter Bourgonje

Universität Potsdam

ISBN 978-3-89838-763-7 (AKA, print)
ISBN 978-1-64368-192-4 (IOS Press, print)
ISBN 978-1-64368-193-1 (IOS Press, online)

Bibliographic information available from the Katalog der Deutschen Nationalbibliothek (German National Library Catalogue) at https://www.dnb.de

Dissertation, approved by Universität Potsdam (University of Potsdam), Humanwissenschaftlichen Fakultät (Faculty of Human Sciences)
Date of the defense: 16 April 2021
Supervisor: Prof. Dr. Manfred Stede
Reviewer: Prof. Dr. Leila Kosseim

ORCID page of the author: orcid.org/0000-0003-3541-0678

Publisher
Akademische Verlagsgesellschaft AKA GmbH, Berlin

Represented by Co-Publisher IOS Press
IOS Press BV
Nieuwe Hemweg 6B
1013 BG Amsterdam
The Netherlands
Tel: +31 20 688 3355
Fax: +31 20 687 0019
email: order@iospress.nl

To my father

Abstract

While the last few decades have seen impressive improvements in several areas in Natural Language Processing, asking a computer to make sense of the discourse of utterances in a text remains challenging. There are several different theories that aim to describe and analyse the coherent structure that a well-written text inhibits. These theories have varying degrees of applicability and feasibility for practical use. Presumably the most data-driven of these theories is the paradigm that comes with the Penn Discourse TreeBank, a corpus annotated for discourse relations containing over 1 million words. Any language other than English however, can be considered a low-resource language when it comes to discourse processing.

This dissertation is about shallow discourse parsing (discourse parsing following the paradigm of the Penn Discourse TreeBank) for German. The limited availability of annotated data for German means the potential of modern, deep-learning based methods relying on such data is also limited. This dissertation explores to what extent machine-learning and more recent deep-learning based methods can be combined with traditional, linguistic feature engineering to improve performance for the discourse parsing task. A pivotal role is played by connective lexicons that exhaustively list the discourse connectives of a particular language along with some of their core properties.

To facilitate training and evaluation of the methods proposed in this dissertation, an existing corpus (the Potsdam Commentary Corpus (Stede and Neumann, 2014)) has been extended and additional data has been annotated from scratch. The approach to end-to-end shallow discourse parsing for German adopts a pipeline architecture (Lin et al., 2014) and either presents the first results or improves over state-of-the-art for German for the individual sub-tasks of the discourse parsing task, which are, in processing order, connective identification, argument extraction and sense classification. The end-to-end shallow discourse parser for German that has been developed for the purpose of this dissertation is open-source and available online.

In the course of writing this dissertation, work has been carried out on several connective lexicons in different languages. Due to their central role and demonstrated usefulness for the methods proposed in this dissertation, strategies are discussed for creating or further developing such lexicons for a particular language, as well as suggestions on how to further increase their usefulness for shallow discourse parsing.

Acknowledgments

When starting to work on my dissertation, one of the things I was looking forward to most, was writing this acknowledgments section. Because of the opportunity to explicitly address and thank all the wonderful people that were kind enough to have me as their company throughout this journey. And because it would mean the end of the journey really was near. As much as I have been looking forward to this though, now that the end is near, and now that I do face the final curtain (Sinatra, 1969), the flip side of both of these coins emerges. First, it means that I have to let go of the work reported on in this manuscript. Second, I must not forget to thank anyone who has, knowingly or unknowingly, contributed to me arriving at this point in my career. Tempted as I am to use the good old cliché of wholeheartedly thanking all without whom this dissertation would have been completed much faster and leaving it at that, though, I decided to sit down, mentally go over the last ten years since I started my career as a linguist, and give it a go.

The journey that led to this point, started with my Bachelor and Master in Linguistics and Computational Linguistics, respectively, at Utrecht University, the Netherlands. Were it not for Arno Bastenhof, Mathieu Klomp and Ben McKay, these years would have been much less interesting and exciting. On my first job after graduating, I landed among a group of people who to this day I can hardly believe were really all together then and there. Maybe it's just me, but I've had a wonderful time at Q-go and in addition to being a highly professional and clever bunch, you were awesome to hang out with. Many thanks go out to Mandy Schiffrin (who kindly offered to proofread and pointed out many minor and less minor flaws in an earlier version of this manuscript), Geert Kloosterman, Fabrice Nauze, Jan van Sas, Begoña Villada Moirón, Margaret Salome and the rest of the Q-Go crowd. It is by all means safe to say that you do not realise how influential these years have been to the rest of my career and life in general.

After some deviations that had sometimes more, sometimes less to do with Computational Linguistics and the road that led to this point in my career (ranging from full-blown, corporate industry jobs to hanging around in the steppe of Siberia), at DFKI I have been very grateful to be in the company of Julián Moreno Schneider, María

González García and Stefan Schaffer. The many exciting things we did that had to do with NLP, and the many more exciting things we did that didn't, made the last five years to a great joy and the occasional relief of work and thesis writing. In addition, I am grateful to the many other great colleagues I was allowed to work with at DFKI, and in particular to Georg Rehm and Felix Sasaki for encouraging me to pursue a PhD and leaving me the time and space to do so.

At Potsdam University, both my days in Golm and the conferences we were able to attend together have been very much livened up by the company of Debopam Das, Berfin Aktaş and Maria Skeppsted. The times we were able to spend together have been truly great. Equally grateful I am for having been around at the same time as Tatjana Scheffler, Vladimir Sidorenko, Robin Schäfer, René Knaebel, Yulia Grishina, Yulia Clausen, and the always helpful and supporting Annett Eßlinger and Ines Mauer. In addition, I was in a position to meet many more wonderful people visiting the Applied Computational Linguistics group, often for a relatively limited period of time. Thanks go out to all those visitors not mentioned in the list above.

I would like to thank Leila Kosseim for taking upon her the role of reviewer for this dissertation.

Special thanks go out to Manfred Stede. It was in Germany where I learned the word "Doktorvater", a concept that does not exist in my native language (Dutch). In addition to always having supported me with all and everything to do with this dissertation, I can truly say that I am happy to have been in the position to pursue my PhD in Germany, thus having the opportunity to extend my professional family with a "Doktorvater" who has inspired me in more dimensions than just the professional one.

Another very special thank you goes out to my family. Thanks for always being there for me whilst supporting me in shaping my own life. Thanks dad, for the many discussions over many great beers, the proof-reading of not just this manuscript, but the many others I have produced over the years, and generally for setting a great example not by saying but by doing. Thanks mom, for the many times where you supported me and allowed me to go out and discover. Thanks for your continued support, especially those times where you may have wished I decided differently. Thanks abi, for the many times we've been in phase and adventuring together, or in counter-phase and each venturing into different parts of the world, but never distanced from each other.

The biggest thank you of them all, however, goes out to Şerife. For running around the globe together. For keeping me down-to-earth in good times, and pulling me back to earth in bad times. For putting up with the restlessness in me that others may not always see, but that you know is there. Thank you.

Finally, I guess that I have to succumb to the temptation of the aforementioned cliché. Most of the people mentioned above have had something to do with my professional life and me getting to this point in it. Of course, there really are many, many more, without whom, this work really would have been finished much faster. I sincerely thank you all for the wonderful delays that make this life so worth while living.

peter

Author's Note

The work reported in this dissertation is the result of approximately three years of research. Much of this work has been carried out in collaboration with many wonderful people, many of whom are listed in the acknowledgments section. Parts of this work have been previously published, and this has been explicitly indicated for every instance. Because this previously published work has been carried out in collaboration with other people (co-authors, as well as student assistants), and has made its way into this dissertation, I decided to use plural pronouns consistently throughout this dissertation. The papers of which I am the first author represent my own work; for the other papers, the order of the authors correspond to their contributions to the work reported on in the respective papers.

Most examples used in this dissertation originate from either the Potsdam Commentary Corpus or the Penn Discourse TreeBank. To save space, every time an example from either of these corpora is used, the file ID where the example comes from is cited, but not the paper relating to the corpus itself. In case a (German) Potsdam Commentary Corpus example is used, the reference is marked with `maz-\d+`, in case an (English) Penn Discourse TreeBank example is used, the reference is marked with `wsj_\d+`, where `\d+` refers to a sequence of digits. The papers that go along with the examples are Stede and Neumann (2014) for the Potsdam Commentary Corpus and Prasad et al. (2008) for the Penn Discourse TreeBank.

In terms of formatting, whenever a word or phrase is referred to in general, that word or phrase is printed in *italics*. Whenever a particular instance of that word or phrase (in a given example) is referred to, that word or phrase is included in "double quotes". In order to make this dissertation understandable for non-German speakers, every time a German word, phrase or example is provided, an attempt is made to provide the most faithful English translation. The only exception to this is the content in the appendices, since this primarily serves to demonstrate file formats.

For several components described in this thesis, typically f-score is used as an evaluation metric. For related work, the corresponding papers do not always specify which type of f-score is used. In cases where explicit reference to f1-score was made in the relevant paper, or if I calculated the metric myself, the term f1-score is used. In the remaining cases, the term f-score is used. A similar confusion may occur when referring to arguments of discourse relations. The Penn Discourse TreeBank terminology uses *Arg1* and *Arg2*, whereas the Potsdam Commentary Corpus uses *extarg* and *intarg* (for external argument and internal argument). Note that *Arg1* corresponds to *extarg* and *Arg2* to *intarg* in all cases, and which term is used, depends on the corpus that is being referred to. For more details, please refer to Chapter 5.

Contents

List of Figures

List of Tables

List of Abbreviations

BERT Bidirectional Encoder Representations from Transformers.

CCR a Cognitive approach to Coherence Relations.
CoNLL Conferences on Natural Language Learning.
CSV Comma-Separated Values.

DiMLex DIscourse Marker LEXicon.

EDU Elementary Discourse Unit.

GUI Graphical User Interface.

JSON JavaScript Object Notation.

NLP Natural Language Processing.

PCC Potsdam Commentary Corpus.
PDTB Penn Discourse TreeBank.

RST Rhetorical Structure Theory.

SDRT Segmented Discourse Representation Theory.

WSJ Wall Street Journal.

XML eXtensible Markup Language.

Chapter 1

Introduction

Different sub-fields of (computational) linguistics typically have their own units they focus on. Phonology operates mostly at the sub-word level (consonants and vowels), morphology deals with (sub-)word units (morphemes) and syntax works with sentences. Our area of interest, *discourse processing* can be characterised as linguistics beyond the sentence level. The underlying assumption is that a text is not a random collection of sentences, but instead exhibits a certain amount of coherence and should be about the same topic, or limited range of topics. In the same way that studying the grammar of a language can contribute to understanding utterances in that language, or generating valid new utterances, studying discourse structure can contribute to text understanding, and equally to the generation of new texts. Research on discourse structure is basically about what makes a text a text.

While on the surface level, texts can be made cohesive by various different mechanisms (for example, the fact that subject and verb have to agree in tense and number, or through use of anaphoric pronouns for an entity and its references), coherence is generally understood to be about the logical relations that the sentences, or propositions expressed by them, have with regard to each other. The uncovering of these relations, either manually or automatically, also referred to as *discourse parsing*, is the main theme of this dissertation.

In our experiments, we restrict the scope to monologue text only (with further domain restrictions explained in Chapter 2), and ignore (written) dialogue and spoken language. Even for monologue texts, discourse parsing is a relatively complex task in Natural Language

Processing (NLP) and, as will be made clear in the following chapters, often relies on multiple other upstream tasks, such as part-of-speech tagging, sentence parsing and semantic interpretation and representation. The result of discourse parsing itself (or sub-tasks thereof), can in turn be used in downstream applications, such as Machine Translation (Meyer and Popescu-Belis, 2012), Text Summarisation (Alemany, 2005) or Argumentation Mining (Kirschner et al., 2015).

1.1. Discourse Processing Theories & Frameworks

There are several different theories or frameworks to explain the coherence relations that are present in texts. The most prominent ones are, in chronological order of their seminal papers:

- Rhetorical Structure Theory (RST, Mann and Thompson (1988))

- a Cognitive Approach to Coherence Relations (CCR, Sanders et al. (1992))

- Segmented Discourse Representation Theory (SDRT, Asher et al. (2003))

- the Penn Discourse TreeBank (PDTB, Prasad et al. (2008))

The specifics of the framework used in this dissertation are explained in more detail in Section 1.3. For now it will suffice to provide a brief summary of each of them here.

In RST, the ultimate goal is to construct a single tree-structure in which the leaves are elementary segments and the nodes represent the relations[1] that leaves or non-terminal nodes have with regard to each other. Crucially, the entire text has to result in one single tree and every segment has to be included in it.

CCR has relatively strong ties to psycho-linguistics and attempts to organise the set of relations a text can exhibit into the four[2] different dimensions (originally called 'cognitive primes') of polarity (positive vs. negative), basic operation (additive vs. causal), source of

---

[1]For this, several relation taxonomies have been used over the years (Carlson et al., 2002; Hovy and Maier, 1993; Knott, 1996; Mann and Thompson, 1988; Rösner and Stede, 1992).

[2]Later, a fifth dimension dealing with temporal order has been added (Evers-Vermeul et al., 2017).

2

coherence (objective vs. subjective) and order of the segments (basic vs. non-basic).

SDRT is grounded in Discourse Representation Theory (Kamp and Reyle, 1993) and extends this with rhetorical relations. It provides a formal account of discourse and the extension is motivated by the fact that the interpretation of utterances in dynamic semantics is not bounded by discourse, which results in over-generating interpretations (an unwanted feature, which is addressed by SDRT, which can be seen as an extension to dynamic semantics).

The PDTB is, first and foremost, a corpus annotated for discourse relations. In the corpus, single coherence or discourse relations are annotated and no commitment is made to overall text structure, or how units larger than individual segments relate to each other. Because of this property, parsing following the PDTB paradigm is also referred to as *shallow discourse parsing*. The PDTB is the framework we are adopting throughout this dissertation. A general overview of the PDTB is provided in Section 1.3. An example of an annotated text following the PDTB framework is included in Appendix A.2, and explained in Section 2.2.2. Chapters 4, 5, 6 and 7 will provide more details with regard to particular sub-tasks of the discourse parsing task. But first, an overview of several discourse parsing systems is provided in the next section.

1.2. Discourse Parsers

Because most corpora annotated for discourse relations follow the RST and PDTB frameworks (Carlson et al. (2002) and Prasad et al. (2008), most notably[3]), these two frameworks have been by far the most popular ones for the development of systems that automatically parse a text for discourse relations, also known as discourse parsers. Examples of RST parsers, working on individual sub-tasks or generating the entire RST tree from plain text, are described in Feng and Hirst (2014); Heilman and Sagae (2015); Hernault et al. (2010); Ji and Eisenstein (2014); Joty et al. (2015); Marcu and Echihabi (2002). Because we focus on shallow discourse parsing, we consider RST parsing outside the scope of this dissertation. We refer to the corresponding papers for more details on these systems, and only discuss shallow discourse parsing here.

---

[3]See Section 2.1 for pointers to more annotated corpora.

An influential approach to shallow discourse parsing, following the PDTB framework, has been introduced by Lin et al. (2014). In both 2015 and 2016, the shallow discourse parsing task featured in the Conferences on Natural Language Learning (CoNLL) shared tasks, resulting in a large number of system submissions (see Xue et al. (2015, 2016) for an overview). The overall best-performing system of 2016 achieved an end-to-end f1-score of 27 on the PDTB. Compared to other typical NLP tasks, such as part-of-speech tagging, Named Entity Recognition and even sentence parsing, which typically have f1-scores in the 90's, (shallow) discourse parsing thus is a complex and challenging task; a claim that is further supported by comparatively low inter-annotator agreement scores. The complexity of the task is partially due to the complexity of the individual sub-tasks (and the fact that it is usually interpreted as a conglomerate of sub-tasks in the first place), and partially due to the Lin et al. (2014) pipeline architecture (and its sensitivity to error propagation) that is used by the vast majority of the parsers that participated in the end-to-end sub-tasks of the 2015 and 2016 shared tasks. While these systems focus on an end-to-end application setup, we note that intermediate results of sub-tasks can already help in improving performance for particular down-stream tasks (Burstein et al., 1998; Hewett et al., 2019; Meyer and Popescu-Belis, 2012; Wang et al., 2012).

Generally, the idea of end-to-end shallow discourse parsing is that the parser takes raw text as input, and outputs discourse relations that are present in the input text, following the PDTB framework. Section 1.3 provides a general overview of the different types of relations that the parser is supposed to extract. For more details on particular parts of these relations (i.e., connectives, arguments or senses), we refer to Chapters 4, 5 or 6, respectively.

1.3. The Penn Discourse TreeBank

There are many different ways to express discourse relations in a text. When presented with example (1), most readers will interpret a conditional relation between the two segments, separated by a comma, based on their semantics alone.[4]

---

[4]We apologise for the somewhat sub-optimal examples (1) and (2). They originate from the lyrics to the referenced song, thereby not adhering to the scope of the rest of the work in this thesis (written monologue texts). However,

(1) Order ten dollars or more, we'll shove it down your throat for free. (Aesop Rock, 2005, *9-5'ers Anthem*)

In other cases, particular words or phrases may explicitly signal a particular relation, such as in (2), where "But" signals a contrastive relation between the two sentences.

(2) There's smoke in my iris. But I painted a sunny day on the insides of my eyelids. (Aesop Rock, 2005, *Battery*)

(1) and (2) respectively represent the most frequent relation types in the Penn Discourse TreeBank (henceforth: PDTB): *implicit* (ca. 40% of all relations) and *explicit* (ca. 45% of all relations) relations (respectively, `Implicit` and `Explicit` in PDTB vocabulary). The difference between the two is the presence or absence of an explicit discourse connective (markers like *but, if, however, because*). Because the set of discourse connectives for a particular language is generally understood to be a closed class (see Section 4.1 for a discussion), a third type of relation is included in the PDTB: the alternative lexicalisation (or `AltLex`, in PDTB vocabulary). Comprising ca. 2% of all relations, these are relations that are lexically marked by something that does not comply with the definition of a connective. An example is included in (3), where the phrase "That compared with" signals a contrastive relation.

(3) Earnings fell to $877 million, or $1.51 a share. That compared with the year-earlier $1.25 billion, or $2.10 a share. (wsj_2155)

These three relation types each consist of two segments, referred to as the two arguments (see Chapter 5 for more details), a particular relation sense (according to the PDTB sense hierarchy, see Chapter 6 for more details), and a connective (see Chapter 4 for more details). For `Explicit` and `AltLex` relations, this is the word or phrase that signals the relation. For `Implicit` relations, crucially, the connective is not there, but annotators were requested to indicate which connective could be inserted, such that the annotation for `Implicit` relations also contains a connective.

---

it was the only opportunity to introduce a reference to the favourite artist of the author of this dissertation, and we hope it serves to demonstrate the purpose of the example.

Furthermore, the PDTB[5] defines the two additional relation types of `EntRel` (for entity relation) and `NoRel` (for no relation). An `EntRel` is annotated when no specific sense from the PDTB sense hierarchy could be assigned, but the two segments speak of the same entities. An example is included in (4).

(4) Six-year-old Pace, based in Aurora, Colo., operates 41 warehouse-club stores. The company had losses for several years before turning profitable in fiscal 1988. (wsj_2163)

A `NoRel` is annotated for instances where no relation between two adjacent sentences could be assigned. An example is included in (5).

(5) Jacobs is an international engineering and construction concern. Total capital investment at the site could be as much as $400 million, according to Intel. (wsj_1081)

`EntRel` and `NoRel` instances in the PDTB only have two arguments and no connective or relation sense.

Recall from Section 1.1 that the PDTB has a strong empirical focus and that the theory of shallow discourse parsing is directly tied to the annotations in its corpus. During annotation of the corpus, first the `Explicit` relations were identified and specified (annotating the two arguments and a relation sense). Subsequently, for all adjacent sentence pairs inside the same paragraph that are not already involved in an explicit relation, one of the four remaining relation types was annotated (`Implicit, AltLex, EntRel, NoRel`)[6].

The PDTB owes its name, as well as its content, to the Penn Treebank (Marcus et al., 1993), and is annotated on a subset of the PTB consisting of Wall Street Journal (WSJ) articles. Because the PDTB is by far the largest resource annotated for discourse relations, many computational approaches to discourse processing are based on the corpus and its framework. Though the "shallow" in shallow discourse parsing strictly refers to the fact that no commitment is made to overall text structure, *shallow discourse parsing* and the PDTB framework practically came to be synonyms.

---

[5]In its 2.0 version. The 3.0 version introduced additional relation types, see Section 2.2.2 for more details.

[6]Again, see Section 2.2.2 for the difference between PDTB versions.

1.4. Dissertation Contributions

This dissertation describes the development of a shallow discourse parser for German. To enable both training and evaluation of the components that make up the shallow discourse parser, an existing corpus has been extended and new data has been collected and annotated from scratch. The procedures and the resulting data are explained in Chapter 2. The discourse parser is designed for end-to-end usage, meaning that plain, unstructured and unannotated text is accepted as input, processed, and returned as output in the form of the discourse relations identified in the input text. The architecture of the discourse parser and its technical details are explained and motivated in Chapter 3. The subsequent chapters follow the pipeline architecture that is explained in Chapter 3.

Chapter 4 deals with the sub-task of connective identification. Chapter 5 deals with discourse argument extraction. Chapter 6 discusses the classification of relation sense for connectives and their arguments. Chapter 7 describes our approach to the classification of implicit relations. The contribution for each of these sub-tasks is in either establishing performance on German in the case that no prior work exists, or in improving over state-of-the-art results for German from earlier work.

Because German can be considered a low-resource language with respect to discourse annotation, a central notion in this dissertation is the combination of machine-learning based methods with linguistic knowledge. The latter, in our case, is encoded in connective lexicons and the work done in the course of this dissertation on such lexicons is explained in Chapter 8.

Finally, Chapter 9 summarises the main findings of this dissertation as well as provides an outlook on possible future work and how to overcome challenges faced during the work performed for this dissertation.

1.5. Structure of Chapters

Chapters 2 to 8 each focus on a specific contribution of this dissertation, and, to the reader familiar with discourse processing, can to a certain extent be read in isolation (though the overall structure and order of chapters in this dissertation is not without reason). Each chapter first briefly explains the sub-topic or sub-task of the particular chapter, and then provides an overview of work specifically related to it. After this, an explanation of our method(s) is provided, followed by a presentation of their corresponding results and a discussion of these results, which, following standard NLP practice, is compared to some baseline approach. For some chapters, particularly Chapters 5 and 7, the component dealing with the sub-task at hand is implemented for English to directly compare to a setup where considerably more training data is available. Chapter 8 slightly deviates from this schema, by providing an overview of connective lexicons currently in existence, explaining the work done during the course of this dissertation on several connective lexicons, and by providing a a description of how such lexicons can be created or further developed. However, Chapter 8 does not include any numerical results. For Chapter 2 to 8, the final section consists of a wrap-up of the key contributions of the chapter.

Chapter 2

Data, Resources and Annotation

Data annotated for a particular domain (i.e news, advertisements, encyclopedia entries), a particular language (e.g., German, English, Korean) and a particular task (e.g., part-of-speech tagging, machine translation, question answering) plays a central role in (applied) computational linguistics, or Natural Language Processing (NLP). This data, annotated by humans, also referred to as "gold standard" data, is taken to be the perfect solution[1] to the task at hand, and is what the purpose-built system is being compared to and/or trained on. Depending on both the type of the problem and the availability of annotated data, an approach based on machine-learning or a rule-based approach may be the optimal strategy (combinations of both are typically referred to as hybrid approaches). A rule-based approach, in the extreme case, only needs annotated data for evaluation. A machine-learning based approach uses the annotations for training as well. In this dissertation, we are implementing a hybrid approach, and in addition to training data and hand-crafted rules, we use a connective lexicon as external knowledge source. The extent to which individual components rely on either data, rules, or this connective lexicon, is explained in Chapters 4, 5, 6 and 7.

In this chapter, we explain the data and the connective lexicon that are used throughout this dissertation. We use the Potsdam Commentary Corpus because it is the largest German corpus annotated for discourse relations, with a smaller corpus described in Versley and

---

[1]The same data should be annotated by multiple annotators, so that inter-annotator agreement can be calculated. This agreement figure then puts an upper-bound on expected performance, putting 'perfect' into perspective.

Gastel (2013), and DiMLex, a German connective lexicon, because it is the only available connective lexicon for German. Both the Potsdam Commentary Corpus and DiMLex are further developed as an important contribution of this dissertation. In addition, we annotated additional data, sourced from Wikipedia and news articles, to expand our scope and enable the investigation of domain transfer impact.

The next sections first discuss similar resources for other languages, then successively cover the Potsdam Commentary Corpus, DiMLex, and the additional annotations on Wikipedia and news data. Parts of this chapter are taken from previously published work (Bourgonje et al., 2017; Bourgonje and Stede, 2018b, 2020b).

2.1. Related Work

A convenient overview of several corpora in different languages and frameworks (including RST, SDRT and the PDTB) is provided in Zeldes et al. (2019, p.98), and also later in Table 4.1 on page 42. Of all the corpora listed there, the corpora following the PDTB paradigm are all considerably larger than the Potsdam Commentary Corpus. The PDTB itself has over 1m tokens and 53,631 annotated discourse relations. The Turkish Discourse Treebank (Zeyrek et al., 2010) contains ca. 400k tokens and 8,483[2] annotations for explicit relations. The Chinese Discourse Treebank (Li et al., 2014) contains ca. 73k tokens and 7,310 annotated relations.

To the best of our knowledge, the only other German corpus annotated for discourse relations is described in Versley and Gastel (2013). This subset of the TüBa-D/Z corpus (Telljohann et al., 2012) contains ca. 22k tokens and 1,458 annotated relations. We use the Potsdam Commentary Corpus in this dissertation, because working on this corpus allows us to capture and correct inconsistencies and generally improve the corpus quality.

Next to annotated data, the other type of resource used in this dissertation is a connective lexicon. Developing both human- and machine-readable connective lexicons (in XML format) started with DiMLex in Stede (2002). Many other languages have followed since (Bourgonje et al., 2018; Das et al., 2018, 2020; Feltracco et al., 2016; Mendes and Lejeune, 2016; Mírovský et al., 2016; Roze et al., 2012)

---

[2]Later extensions have been described in Zeyrek and Kurfalı (2017), but additional annotations were done on 10% of the original corpus only.

and a platform hosting these lexicons, enabling (multi-lingual) search by surface forms, categories and other characteristics, is described in Stede et al. (2019) and available online[3]. We refer to Section 4.1 for our definition of connectives and the criteria for including items in such a lexicon. In this dissertation, we are using DiMLex because it is the only connective lexicon for German. Several other lexicons have been either created or further developed in the course of this dissertation, however. See Chapter 8 for more information.

2.2. The Potsdam Commentary Corpus

2.2.1. Versions 1 to 2.1

The Potsdam Commentary Corpus (henceforth: PCC), first introduced in Stede (2004), is a collection of news commentary articles from a regional German newspaper (the *Märkische Allgemeine Zeitung*[4]), originally annotated for part-of-speech information, syntax, rhetorical structure, connectives and co-reference. Essentially, the corpus was constructed to study text structure (in the spirit of RST), and the multi-layer characteristic was introduced to allow investigation into the ways in which text structure and other linguistic structures, such as sentence-level syntax and information structure, interact. The different layers have been annotated in a largely independent manner and annotation guidelines were designed to work on plain, non-augmented text, such that correlations between the layers can be explored *a posteriori*. The domain of news commentary was selected because articles of this kind can be expected to exhibit argumentative structures interesting for the original task of studying text structure, and the authors are typically trained or professional writers.

Over the years, the annotations have been improved upon and extended, and the 2.0 version and its updates are described in Stede and Neumann (2014). With the 2.0 version, syntax remained unchanged, but the co-reference annotation guidelines were largely rewritten and all co-reference annotations were checked against the new guidelines. In addition, the RST trees have been checked against the rewritten

---

[3]http://connective-lex.info/
[4]https://www.maz-online.de/

annotation guidelines, which contained suggestions for nuclearity assignment and attachment points for sub-trees. Finally, the 2.0 version saw a new layer of connectives and their arguments in the spirit of the PDTB. While this layer resembles the shallow discourse relation paradigm as discussed in Chapter 1, it differs from the PDTB annotations in two crucial ways. First, it only includes relations that are explicitly signalled by a connective, following the adapted definition[5] of Pasch et al. (2003), and thus ignores implicit relations and other relation types defined in the PDTB (such as alternative lexicalisations and entity relations, see Section 2.2.2). Second, relation senses for connectives and their arguments were not annotated.

The 2.1 update, described in Bourgonje and Stede (2018b), includes a new layer of *aboutness topics* (Jacobs, 2001), automatically produced dependency trees following the universal dependencies scheme in its 2.3 version (Nivre et al., 2018) and some bug fixes. In addition, format conversions were done to upload the corpus in ANNIS[6], a tool specifically targeted at searching and visualising linguistic corpora annotated on multiple layers (Krause and Zeldes, 2016).

The PCC is publicly available and can be downloaded from the corpus website[7] or viewed in a public installation of ANNIS[8].

2.2.2. Version 2.2

The 2.2 version is the version of the corpus we are using throughout this dissertation. This important update to the corpus, and a key contribution of this dissertation, is the extension of the connectives and arguments layer. While this layer resembles the shallow discourse annotations of the PDTB, earlier versions differed in two important ways, as described in Section 2.2.1. This has been addressed in the 2.2 version, in which additional relation types were annotated, following the PDTB2.0 guidelines (Prasad et al., 2007). The following four relation types were added:

- **Implicit**, for adjacent sentences inside the same paragraph that were not yet connected by an explicit discourse connective. See example (1) from Section 1.3.

---

[5]See section 4.1 for the actual definition.
[6]https://korpling.german.hu-berlin.de/annis3/
[7]http://angcl.ling.uni-potsdam.de/resources/pcc.html
[8]The ANNIS installation hosts the 2.1 version.

- **AltLex**, or alternative lexicalisation, for cases where the relation is overtly realised, but not by a proper connective. Examples from the PCC are "Hinzu kommt" (*In addition*), "Aus taktischen Gründen" (*For tactical reasons*) and "Neben" (*Next to*).

- **EntRel**, or entity relation, for cases where no particular relation sense could be inferred, but coherence between the segments was established based on them speaking of the same entities. See example (4) from Section 1.3.

- **NoRel**, or no relation, for cases where no relation between two adjacent sentences (inside the same paragraph) could be inferred. See example (5) from Section 1.3.

With regard to relation types, the PDTB3.0 added several new relation types, of which intra-sentential implicit relations are probably the most frequent ones. To annotate these in the PCC as well would have led to considerably more annotation effort, which was not feasible for the purpose of this dissertation, so we restricted ourselves to the PDTB2.0 relation type inventory.

The second dimension of extension for the 2.2 version is the annotation of relation senses, i.e., what specific *kind* of relation is expressed by the two arguments (and the connective or alternative lexicalisation, if present). For this, we did follow the PDTB3.0 guidelines and adopted the corresponding sense hierarchy (see Webber et al. (2019, p.17) or Section 6.2). This hierarchy distinguishes four main classes on the first level (Temporal, Comparison, Contingency and Expansion), sub-divided into 17 types[9] on the second level, in turn sub-divided into 23 sub-types on the third, most detailed level of sub-types. The third level adds information about the order of the arguments for those relations that are asymmetric and is left blank for symmetric relations.

In addition to the extra annotations, in the 2.2 version the inline XML format of the connectives and arguments layer has been replaced with standoff XML for more convenient automated processing. Listing 2.1 illustrates the pre-2.2 inline XML format; Listing 2.2 illustrates the same relation in standoff XML format. This standoff format is divided into a first section containing all the tokens along with

---

[9]The +/- belief and speechAct add-ons are typically interpreted as additional features, not as types on their own.

their unique ID, and a section containing all annotated relations, of which Listing 2.2 displays one example. Every relation contains an `id`, `pdtb3_sense` and `type` as attributes and is furthermore divided into `connective_tokens`, `ext_arg_token` and `int_arg_tokens` nodes. Both argument nodes contain the corresponding token IDs and the tokens themselves for human reading convenience. For explicit relations and alternative lexicalisations, the connective node contains the corresponding tokens and their IDs. For implicit relations, the connective that could semantically be inserted (following the PDTB annotation guidelines) is contained in the `connective_tokens` node, but without an ID, because the token is not present in the text. For `EntRel` and `NoRel` relations, the `connective_tokens` node is present, but left empty. A full example is included in Appendix A. Appendix A.1 displays the plain (tokenised) text format of one single file. Appendix A.2 contains a visualisation of the discourse relations in this file, marking, in subscript, where the connective (if applicable) and both arguments start and end. Note that the type of relation and the relation sense are not included in this visualisation. For this, we refer to the XML file included in Appendix A.3, which includes all information related to the discourse relation annotation layer of the corresponding file.

Listing 2.1: PCC2.0 connectives and arguments excerpt

```
Und FDP–Luftikus Jürgen W. Möllemann bereist seinerseits schon jetzt
    eifrig den Nahen Osten , um
<unit type="ext" id="5">
    für diesen Fall gerüstet zu sein
</unit>
<unit type="int" id="5">
    <connective id="5" relation="addition">und</connective>
    sich als neuer liberaler Außenminister zu empfehlen .
</unit>
```

Listing 2.2: PCC2.2 discourse annotation excerpt

```
<relation relation_id="5" pdtb3_sense="Expansion.Conjunction" type="
    explicit">
  <connective_tokens>
    <connective_token id="62" token="und"/>
  </connective_tokens>
  <ext_arg_tokens>
    <ext_arg_token id="56" token="für"/>
    <ext_arg_token id="57" token="diesen"/>
    <ext_arg_token id="58" token="Fall"/>
    <ext_arg_token id="59" token="gerüstet"/>
    <ext_arg_token id="60" token="zu"/>
    <ext_arg_token id="61" token="sein"/>
  </ext_arg_tokens>
  <int_arg_tokens>
    <int_arg_token id="62" token="und"/>
    <int_arg_token id="63" token="sich"/>
    <int_arg_token id="64" token="als"/>
    <int_arg_token id="65" token="neuer"/>
    <int_arg_token id="66" token="liberaler"/>
    <int_arg_token id="67" token="Außenminister"/>
    <int_arg_token id="68" token="zu"/>
    <int_arg_token id="69" token="empfehlen"/>
    <int_arg_token id="70" token="."/>
  </int_arg_tokens>
</relation>
```

The following subsection provides an overview and some statistics of the PCC2.2. Subsequently, we describe the procedures followed to obtain the new annotations, and the resulting inter-annotator agreement is explained.

2.2.2.1. Corpus Statistics

The PCC2.2 consists of 176 articles, containing 33,222 words. Table 2.1 illustrates the distribution of relations over the entire corpus.

Because the PDTB annotation guidelines are adopted, Figure 2.1 compares our distribution of relation types to the PDTB2.0 (Prasad et al., 2008). In terms of relation types, the PCC2.2 roughly follows the distribution of the PDTB2.0, with the most striking difference being the smaller number of EntRel relations (2.5% in the PCC vs. 12.8% in the PDTB). Furthermore it has more Explicit relations

	PCC2.2
AltLex	96
EntRel	56
Explicit	1,112
Implicit	905
NoRel	35
Total	**2,204**

Table 2.1: Distribution of relations in the PCC2.2

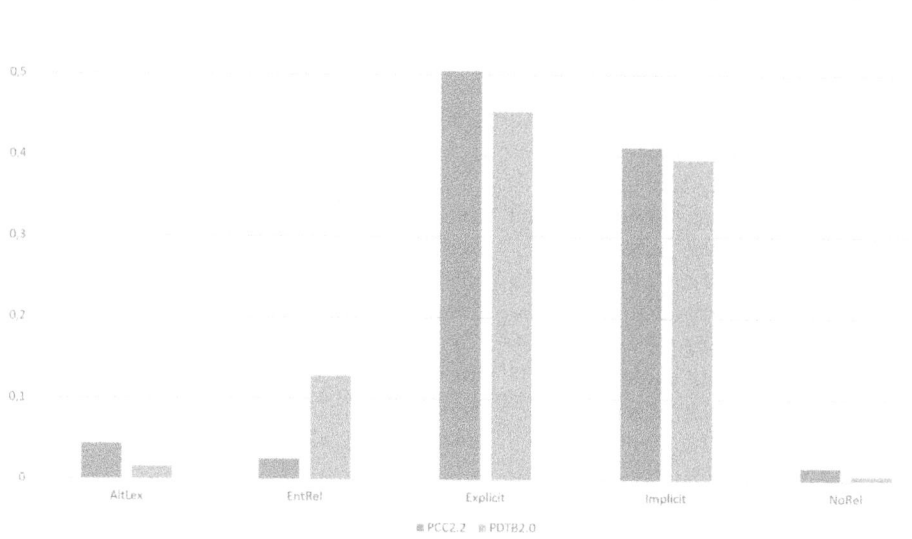

Figure 2.1: Relative distribution of relations in PCC2.2 and PDTB2.0

(50.5% vs. 45.5%) and AltLex relations (4.4% vs. 1.5%). The difference in number of EntRel relations could be due to the particular Wall Street Journal-style (the PDTB texts are all WSJ articles). The financial news articles of the WSJ often makes mention of management successions, which are typically annotated as EntRel relations. An example is included in (6):

(6) Mr. Wertheimer, 38 years old, had been a first vice president in the industrial group in investment banking. He succeeds Everett Meyers, who resigned in May. (wsj_2028)

Another factor could be the text length. The average length of one article in the PCC is 189 words, whereas the average PDTB article has 455 words. The authors featuring in the PCC may have felt the need to be concise, and thus may have chosen to use fewer `EntRel` constructions. More research on the impact of text length on discourse structure would be needed to verify this, though. For this, the current corpus may not be sufficient, as the PCC only has 56 `EntRel` instances in total.

Figure 2.2 compares the distribution of the four top-level senses of the PCC and the PDTB. For more detailed graphs, we refer to Chapters 6 and 7. The distribution of senses in the PCC resembles that of the distribution in the PDTB, with a slightly larger difference for temporal relations (7.0% in the PCC vs.13.1% in the PDTB). An

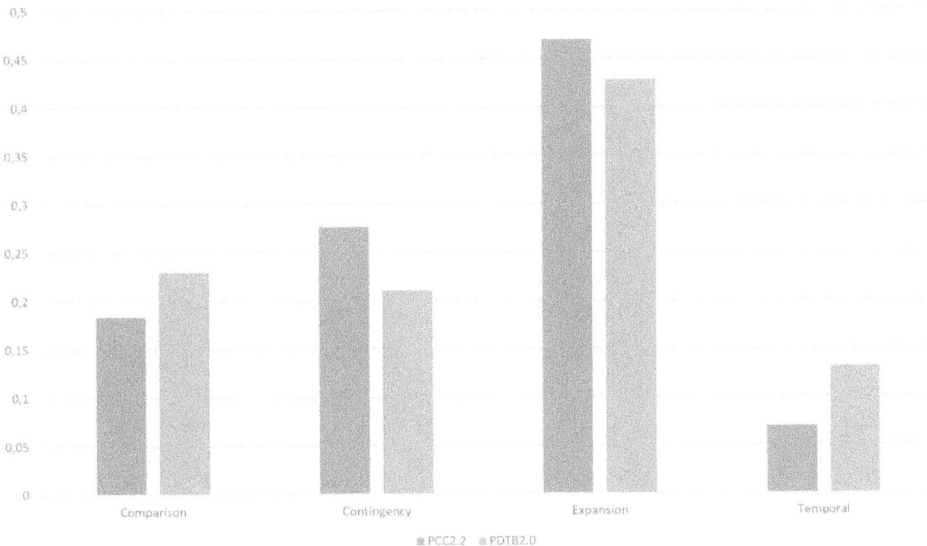

Figure 2.2: Relative distribution of top-level class senses in the PCC2.2 and PDTB2.0

explanation for this difference could be the news domain of the PDTB vs. the news commentary domain of the PCC. Mentioning events and when they took place is more relevant in proper news, than it is in commentary on news events, which could explain the difference in number of temporal relations.

Zooming in on individual relation types (`Explicit`, `Implicit` and `AltLex` cases[10]), again when considering the four top-level senses, the PCC roughly matches the PDTB for `Explicit` and `Implicit` (Figures 2.3 and 2.4), but considerably deviates for `AltLex` cases (Figure

---

[10]`EntRel` and `NoRel` instances by definition have no sense assigned to them.

2.5). In the latter, especially relations of the contingency class are much less frequent (9.4% vs. 44.3%), mostly at the expense of temporal class relations (37.5% vs. 13.8%). A more detailed analysis led to no obvious reason for this discrepancy, though we note that the AltLex comparison is based on only 96 instances in the PCC, rendering the comparison less significant than the Explicit (1,112 in the PCC) and Implicit (905 in the PCC) comparisons.

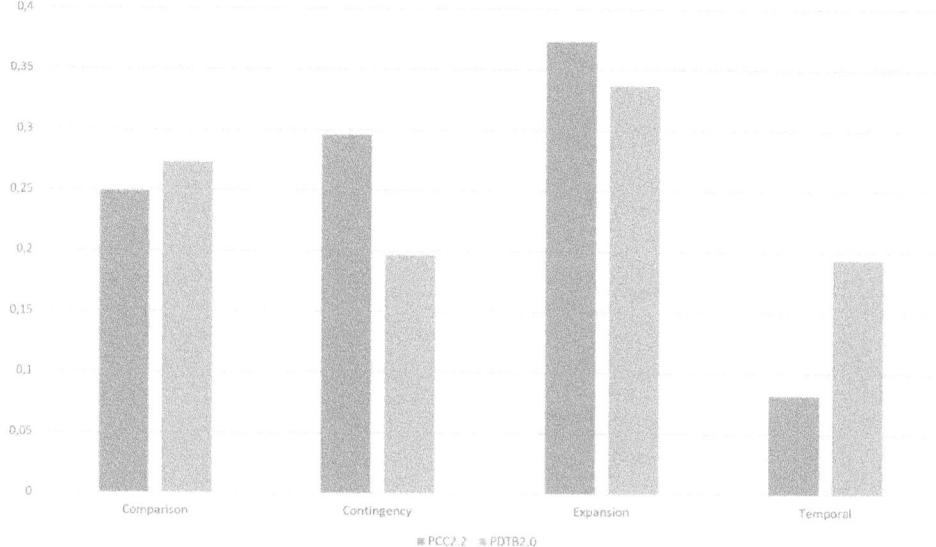

Figure 2.3: Relative sense distribution of explicit relations in the PCC2.2 and PDTB2.0

Table 2.1 and Figures 2.1 to 2.5 relate to the additional annotations of the PCC2.2. In the following chapters, subsections are included providing more details on the characteristics of the PCC with regard to connectives (Section 4.3), arguments (Section 5.2) and senses for explicit (Section 6.2) and implicit (Section 7.2) relations.

The next section explains the annotation procedures used to obtain the additional annotations, and their corresponding inter-annotator agreement numbers.

2.2.3. Annotation Procedure & Inter-Annotator Agreement

This section is divided into two parts, of which the first covers the annotation of additional relation types, and the second the annotation of relation senses.

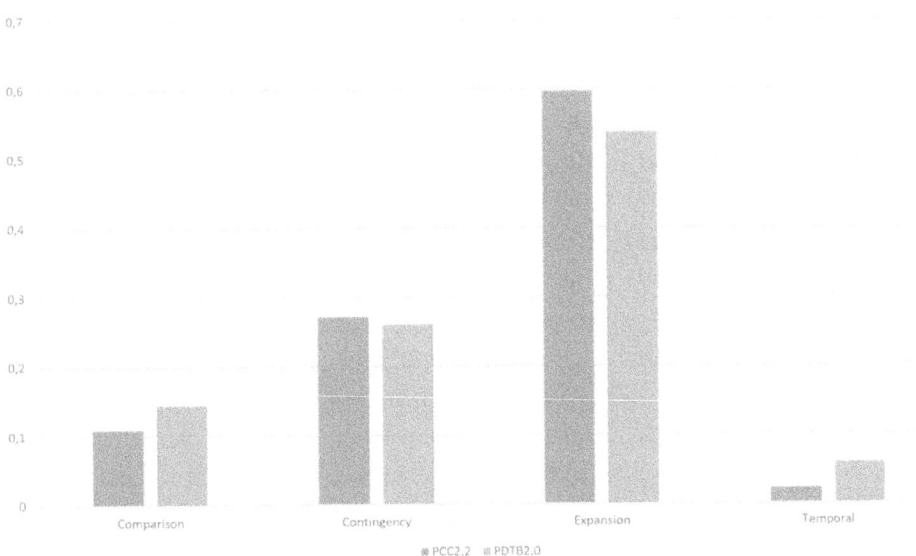

Figure 2.4: Relative sense distribution of implicit relations in the PCC2.2 and PDTB2.0

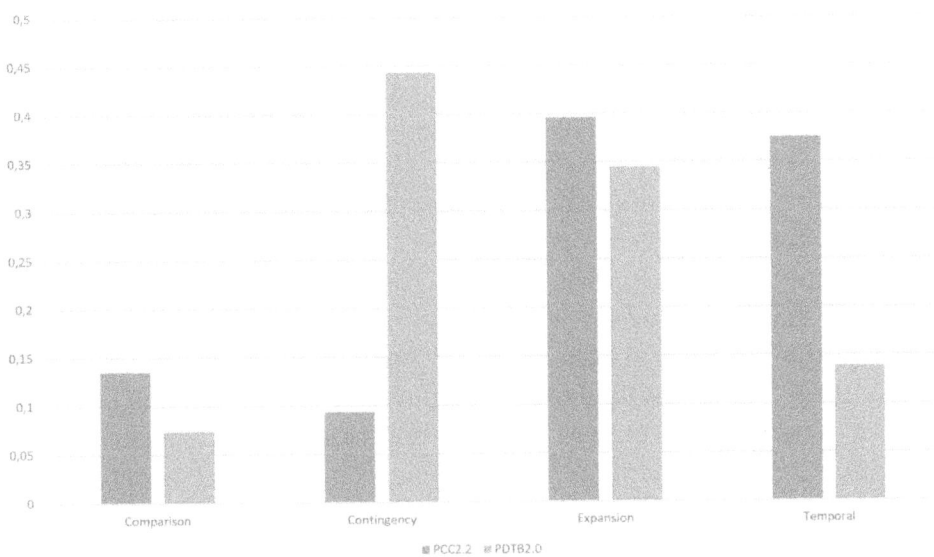

Figure 2.5: Relative sense distribution of AltLex relations in the PCC2.2 and PDTB2.0

2.2.3.1. Relation Type Annotation

Since the PCC2.1 already contained explicit relations[11], we proceeded with the annotation of the additional four relation types from the PDTB2.0 as explained earlier; `Implicit`, `AltLex`, `EntRel` and `NoRel` cases. One of these four relation types was annotated for all adjacent sentences that were not already connected by an explicit connective. I.e., if the external argument of an explicit relation is some sentence A or part thereof and the connective and the internal argument is in some sentence B or part thereof, the sentence pair A-B was skipped. Consider example (7), where the last clause of the first sentence ("ärgerlich ist es trotzdem.") and the second sentence ("Und aberwitzig dazu.") are involved in a relation. Therefore, no further relation was annotated between these two sentences.

(7) Dass die beiden geladenen Jugendlichen im Laufe des Abends immer weniger zu Wort kamen, war sicher keine böse Absicht, *ärgerlich ist es trotzdem.* <u>Und</u> **aberwitzig dazu.** (maz_11299) *The fact that the two invited young people had less and less to say during the course of the evening was certainly not a bad intention, but it is annoying nevertheless. And ludicrous.*

A further constraint, following the PDTB scheme, is that the sentence pair has to be within the same paragraph. Consider Figure 2.6 (further explained below), where the initial sentence pair "Auf Eis gelegt" (*Put on hold*) and "Dagmar Ziegler sitzt in der Schuldenfalle." (*Dagmar Ziegler is in debt.*) is skipped because of the paragraph boundary between them. Paragraph segmentation of the PCC was done based on layout, effectively splitting on double newlines. Because the adjacent sentences were considered to be the two arguments of the relation and arguments spanning more than one sentence are not considered, argument span annotation was redundant.

The original connectives and arguments layer was annotated with ConnAnno, a tool specifically designed for the purpose (Stede and Heintze, 2004). This tool however, is based on the detection of (potential) connectives and therefore is not suitable for the annotation of non-explicit relations. The tool used to annotate the PDTB, the PDTB Annotator (Lee et al., 2016) does cover all relation types we are interested in. However, due to the different XML format of the

---

[11]Without a relation sense still, see next subsection.

PCC, a conversion would be needed to accommodate using this tool. Since we had partial annotations already, starting from scratch on the plain text would mean having to annotate the explicit relations again, or merging them at later stage, requiring the same conversion.

Instead, we exported the entire corpus and its existing annotations to CSV format (one file per article) and loaded this into a spreadsheet editor and configured conditional formatting. Figure 2.6 displays what the annotator would see. The pre-existing annotations for explicit relations were greyed out. For adjacent sentences in the same paragraph (split by empty rows), the type and, if applicable (for implicit relations and alternative lexicalisations) sense and connective had to be specified. After annotation, a series of consistency checks were performed to capture typographical errors or other inconsistencies (such as implicit relations without a sense). Finally, the CSV format was converted back into the standoff XML format (see Figure 2.2).

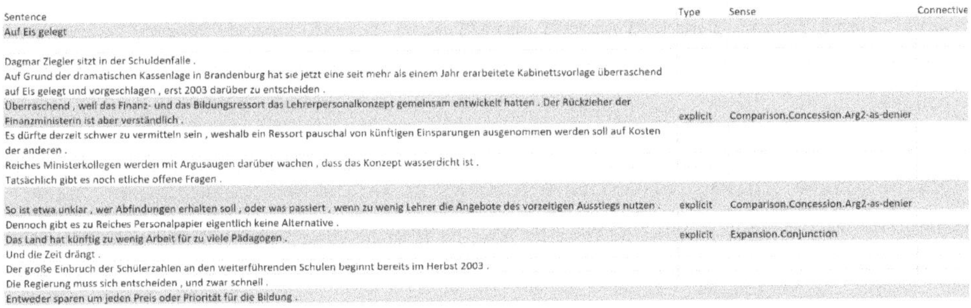

Sentence	Type	Sense	Connective
Auf Eis gelegt			
Dagmar Ziegler sitzt in der Schuldenfalle .			
Auf Grund der dramatischen Kassenlage in Brandenburg hat sie jetzt eine seit mehr als einem Jahr erarbeitete Kabinettsvorlage überraschend auf Eis gelegt und vorgeschlagen , erst 2003 darüber zu entscheiden .			
Überraschend , weil das Finanz- und das Bildungsressort das Lehrerpersonalkonzept gemeinsam entwickelt hatten . Der Rückzieher der Finanzministerin ist aber verständlich .	explicit	Comparison.Concession.Arg2-as-denier	
Es dürfte derzeit schwer zu vermitteln sein , weshalb ein Ressort pauschal von künftigen Einsparungen ausgenommen werden soll auf Kosten der anderen .			
Reiches Ministerkollegen werden mit Argusaugen darüber wachen , dass das Konzept wasserdicht ist .			
Tatsächlich gibt es noch etliche offene Fragen .			
So ist etwa unklar , wer Abfindungen erhalten soll , oder was passiert , wenn zu wenig Lehrer die Angebote des vorzeitigen Ausstiegs nutzen .	explicit	Comparison.Concession.Arg2-as-denier	
Dennoch gibt es zu Reiches Personalpapier eigentlich keine Alternative .			
Das Land hat künftig zu wenig Arbeit für zu viele Pädagogen .	explicit	Expansion.Conjunction	
Und die Zeit drängt .			
Der große Einbruch der Schülerzahlen an den weiterführenden Schulen beginnt bereits im Herbst 2003 .			
Die Regierung muss sich entscheiden , und zwar schnell .			
Entweder sparen um jeden Preis oder Priorität für die Bildung .			

Figure 2.6: Screenshot of CSV annotation format

The author of this dissertation annotated the entire PCC for additional relation types. To obtain inter-annotator agreement figures, a second annotator, familiar with both discourse relation annotation and the PDTB guidelines beforehand, annotated a subset of 20 randomly selected PCC articles (just over 10% of the entire corpus). This resulted in a Cohen's Kappa of .28. Our particular annotation setup, annotating only non-explicit relations, renders a direct comparison to competitors impossible. Others however report a considerably higher agreement for the full annotation task (including explicit relations) and Zeyrek et al. (2020) report an agreement of .78. Prasad et al. (2008) report agreement figures for argument spans and senses, but not for relation types. Upon manual investigation, we found that the most frequent case of disagreement was between `Implicit` and `EntRel` relations. In (8), a typical example is illustrated.

(8) Mit Helga Kaden streicht eine der namhaftesten Geschäftsleute der Stadt die Segel. Sie konnte ihr traditionsreiches Geschäft wegen der anhaltenden Kundenflaute nicht mehr über Wasser halten. (maz-18914)
With Helga Kaden calling it a day, one of the most well-known entrepreneurs of the city is gone. She could not keep her business aloft, due to a diminishing customer base.

The second sentence contains an explicit relation, providing the reason for the bankruptcy. Since this is completely internal to the second sentence though, the relation to be annotated was between the first and the second sentence. One annotator interpreted an `EntRel`, on the basis of the two sentences being about the same entity ("Helga Kaden" in the first sentence, referred to by the pronoun "Sie" ("she") in the second sentence. The other annotator interpreted this sequence as an `Implicit` relation, with an *Expansion.Level-of-detail.Arg2-as-detail* sense, and "genauer gesagt" (*more precisely*) as implicit connective.

Another frequent case of disagreement with regard to relation type was between implicit relations and alternative lexicalisations, where one annotator consistently interpreted a semi-colon as alternative lexicalisation, whereas the other annotator did not. In both our definition and the PDTB framework, semi-colons are excluded from the definition of connectives, but whether or not they can be interpreted as alternative lexicalisations is not explicitly addressed in the annotation guidelines.

2.2.3.2. Relation Sense Annotation

The relation types for which a relation sense is specified according to PDTB guidelines (`Explicit`, `Implicit` and `AltLex`), were subsequently annotated for their relation sense. Because we followed the PDTB paradigm thusfar, we also adopt the corresponding sense taxonomy. And because adopting the most recent PDTB3.0 version of this sense hierarchy (Webber et al., 2019, p.17) did not incur any additional annotation efforts (compared to using the PDTB2.0 version), we used the most recent version. After familiarising themselves with the PDTB3.0 sense hierarchy, the annotators were instructed to first read the entire article (on average ca. 189 words) to understand the context. After this, going through the individual relations, the relevant sense had to be selected from the sense inventory. In the case of ambiguous relations, the annotators were encouraged to note this down in a comment, but required to enter only the one sense that was most prominent to them in the relevant field.

For the same reasons we did not use ConnAnno or the PDTB Annotator earlier (partially annotated data and/or incompatible annotation formats), we did not use it here. Instead of exporting to CSV though, this time the annotator was asked to open the PCC files in an XML editor of choice and specify the relevant sense attribute for explicit and implicit relations and alternative lexicalisations. Figure 2.7 displays what the annotator would see. The relation sense had to be specified in the **pdtb3_sense** attribute of the relation node. After

```xml
<relation relation_id="5" pdtb3_sense="INSERT_SENSE_HERE">
  <connective_tokens>
    <connective_token id="61" token="aber"/>
  </connective_tokens>
  <ext_arg_tokens>
    <ext_arg_token id="42" token="Überraschend"/>
    <ext_arg_token id="43" token=","/>
    <ext_arg_token id="44" token="weil"/>
    <ext_arg_token id="45" token="das"/>
    <ext_arg_token id="46" token="Finanz-"/>
    <ext_arg_token id="47" token="und"/>
    <ext_arg_token id="48" token="das"/>
    <ext_arg_token id="49" token="Bildungsressort"/>
    <ext_arg_token id="50" token="das"/>
    <ext_arg_token id="51" token="Lehrerpersonalkonzept"/>
    <ext_arg_token id="52" token="gemeinsam"/>
    <ext_arg_token id="53" token="entwickelt"/>
    <ext_arg_token id="54" token="hatten"/>
    <ext_arg_token id="55" token="."/>
  </ext_arg_tokens>
  <int_arg_tokens>
    <int_arg_token id="56" token="Der"/>
    <int_arg_token id="57" token="Rückzieher"/>
    <int_arg_token id="58" token="der"/>
    <int_arg_token id="59" token="Finanzministerin"/>
    <int_arg_token id="60" token="ist"/>
    <int_arg_token id="61" token="aber"/>
    <int_arg_token id="62" token="verständlich"/>
    <int_arg_token id="63" token="."/>
  </int_arg_tokens>
</relation>
```

Figure 2.7: Screenshot of XML annotation format

annotation, a series of consistency checks were again performed to catch typographical and other errors.

The author of this dissertation annotated the entire PCC for relation senses. To obtain inter-annotator agreement figures, a second annotator, familiar with both the annotation of discourse relations and the PDTB sense hierarchy beforehand, annotated a subset of 17 articles, containing 108 relations (approx. 10% of the entire corpus). This subset was extracted to mirror the distribution of top-level senses[12] of the entire corpus.

The resulting agreement on the second level of the sense hierarchy was 82.4%, with Cohen's Kappa at .87. Agreement on the most detailed, third level of the sense hierarchy was 70.4%, with Cohen's Kappa at .74. Prasad et al. (2008) report an agreement of 80% on the third level and 84% on the second level. Versley and Gastel (2013), in their two pilot studies, report Cohen's Kappa values of .65 and .69 for the second level of the PDTB sense hierarchy. To the best of our knowledge, the only other publication reporting on PDTB sense annotation agreement in particular is Zhou and Xue (2015), who created a PDTB corpus for Chinese and report an agreement of 84.5%, noting that they *lump the finer-grained semantic types together into the coarser-grained semantic classes before performing the computation* (Zhou and Xue, 2015, p.426). This presumably relates to first level agreement, which in our case is at least 82.4% (we only computed agreement for the second and third level).

The double-annotated subset of the data (108 relations) was too small to draw any conclusions on particular sense pairs being more difficult to distinguish than others[13], since the vast majority of disagreement instances were singletons.

2.3. DiMLex

First introduced in Stede (2002), DiMLex is a German lexicon of discourse connectives packaged in an easily (machine-)readable XML format. Since its introduction in 2002, it has been populated and further developed using different methods, including extracting entries from annotated data, adding entries from intuition (a native speaker's knowledge of the possible uses of the connective) and adding entries

---

[12]Extracting a subset this size that reflected the sense distribution down to a more detailed level was impossible since some detailed senses had very low frequency or were unique in the corpus.

[13]For example, the distinction between *contrast* and *concession* is known to pose challenges to annotators (Prasad et al., 2007).

resulting from bi-lingual projection, of a lexicon in a different language in combination with a parallel corpus. Its most recent official update, described in Scheffler and Stede (2016), led to a lexicon with 275 entries, each entry provided with syntactic and semantic information, orthographic variants, ambiguity information (both with regard to connective reading and relation sense) and other types of information.

An example entry is shown in Listing 2.3 for *also* (*therefore, well, so*). The `orths` node lists orthographic variants and for each lists whether or not it is the canonical form. Surface form information (number of tokens, i.e., single for single words, phrasal for multiple words, and continuous or discontinuous) is also stored here. The `ambiguity` node specifies whether the connective can have both sentential and discourse reading or discourse reading only, and in case of the former, whether it can represent multiple senses in the PDTB3.0 sense hierarchy. The `focuspart` node specifies whether or not this connective allows for associated focus particles. The `non_conn_reading` provides examples of non-connective reading in the case that this connective can have a sentential reading. The `stts` node displays part-of-speech tags[14]. The `syn` node lists the syntactic information (syntactic category, order of the arguments) and semantic (nested in the `sem` node; relation sense) information for this connective. For all entries, the relevant information is provided and irrelevant fields can be left blank. The lexicon documentation as well as the lexicon itself are available in the DiMLex repository[15].

---

[14]The corpus frequencies originate from an unpublished annotation effort and are not used in this dissertation.

[15]https://github.com/discourse-lab/dimlex

Listing 2.3: Example entry in DiMLex

```
<entry id="k6" word="also">
    <orths>
        <orth type="cont" canonical="1" onr="k6o1">
            <part type="single">also</part>
        </orth>
        <orth type="cont" canonical="0" onr="k6o2">
            <part type="single">Also</part>
        </orth>
    </orths>
    <ambiguity>
        <non_conn freq="9" anno_N="23">1</non_conn>
        <sem_ambiguity>0</sem_ambiguity>
    </ambiguity>
    <focuspart>0</focuspart>
    <non_conn_reading>
        <example>Also gut!</example>
        <example>Na also.</example>
    </non_conn_reading>
    <stts/>
    <syn>
        <cat>konnadv</cat>
        <integr/>
        <ordering>
            <ante>0</ante>
            <post>1</post>
            <insert>0</insert>
        </ordering>
        <sem>
            <pdtb3_relation sense="cause-result" freq="14" anno_N="
                14"/>
        </sem>
    </syn>
</entry>
```

Because DiMLex has been worked on and improved upon over the course of many years, it can be considered a relatively stable and exhaustive resource. In the course of the work performed for this dissertation, only minor modifications to the lexicon have been made. Most of these were the by-product of connective lexicon generation and development work targeted at languages other than German, which is discussed in Chapter 8.

Throughout the work described in the following chapters, DiMLex is used as a resource for lexical look-up.

2.4. Wikipedia & News Data

We annotated additional data, both to establish the impact of domain transfer and to improve the performance of connective identification in general. The data used for annotation was sourced with a specific list of seed connectives. This seed list consisted of connectives that proved difficult to disambiguate in earlier work (Bourgonje and Stede, 2018a), i.e., had an f1-score of <0.70, or that did not appear at all in the PCC (but are listed in DiMLex). The domains were Wikipedia and news articles, both selected for their large size; with some connectives being very rare, we needed a large corpus in order to maximise the chances to sample a sufficient number. We downloaded a dump of the German Wikipedia from February 2018 and the news articles were taken from a German-English parallel corpus[16].

2.4.1. Sampling & Annotation Procedure

Using this data, we sampled instances of potential connectives from the seed list to annotate them according to function (i.e., discourse vs. sentential reading) and also sense (i.e., particular sense in the PDTB hierarchy). The seed list contained 42 connectives scoring below our 0.70 f1-score threshold, and 162 connectives from DiMLex that are not present in the PCC, amounting to a set of 204 connectives. For each connective in this seed list, we sampled up to 20 instances in total from both corpora; 10 from the news texts and 10 from Wikipedia. Because the Wikipedia corpus was considerably larger than the news texts, if no 10 instances of a seed could be found in the news texts, we selected more from Wikipedia to arrive at 20 instances. Despite its considerable size, the Wikipedia corpus was also not always large enough to sample 20 instances. Some connectives, like "in Anbetracht dessen" (*considering that*), "sintemal" (*because*) and "umso mehr als" (*all the more since*) are very rare and no 20 instances could be found. In total, we ended up with 3,124 connective candidates. Chapters 4 and 6 include more information about the distribution of connectives and senses in this data.

---

[16]http://homepages.inf.ed.ac.uk/pkoehn/publications/de-news/

For every connective candidate found, we included the sentence it appeared in, the five preceding sentences and the two following sentences (unless the candidate was at the start or end of the document, in which case we took everything up till the start or end). This context was included to allow the annotator to better understand the context of the connective candidate. Based on the external argument distributions in the PCC (see Table 5.4), this maximises chances of including both the potential connective's arguments.

For every instance, the annotator had to specify if it had either sentential or discourse reading, and in the case of the latter, specify the sense. Since at time of annotation, the PDTB3.0 was not yet released, we used the PDTB2.0 version of the sense hierarchy and later converted this to PDTB3.0 senses. Note that this deviates from our annotation guidelines for the PCC2.2, and here, only connectives and their senses are annotated and other PDTB relation types are ignored.

Because the procedure concerned annotating plain text, we adopted the annotation procedure of Stede and Neumann (2014) and used ConnAnno (Stede and Heintze, 2004) as annotation tool. In ConnAnno, potential connectives are automatically highlighted through pattern matching, and the annotator has to indicate sentential or discourse reading, and the relevant sense has to be selected from a drop-down menu. The argument spans are automatically suggested based on punctuation. Because we were primarily interested in connectives and senses for this annotation effort, and because it can be relatively tedious to check and correct argument spans (using the cursor in the interface), we instructed the annotators to skip this step in the interest of speed. The extra sentences (five before, two after) around the connective's sentence that we extracted from the Wikipedia and news texts as context, could also contain connectives, which then would be highlighted and considered by ConnAnno. We instructed the annotators to skip these though, and annotate only the connective of interest, which was typographically marked in the input (i.e., surrounded by a double asterisk), and later removed from the XML output format. A screenshot of what the annotator would see is included in Figure 2.8, with the connective candidate highlighted in red, and the drop-down menu displaying the two possible senses for this connective.

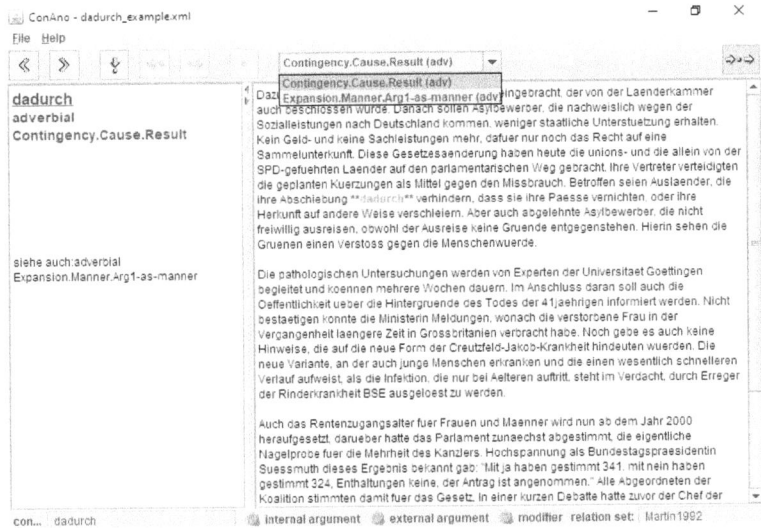

Figure 2.8: Screenshot of ConnAnno GUI

2.4.2. Inter-Annotator Agreement

The entire set of 3,124 instances was annotated by the author of this dissertation, and a subset was annotated by a second annotator (the same as in 2.2.3.2) to obtain inter-annotator agreement scores. In 64.6% of cases (cohen's Kappa of .30), both annotators agreed on the candidate's function (being either a connective or not a connective). For the PCC2.0, Stede and Neumann (2014) report an agreement of 74.5% for this task, and this figure compares to the .28 Kappa value for our annotation campaign on the PCC (see Section 2.2.3.1), though as indicated above, the PCC2.2 annotation effort was targeted at annotating non-explicit relations, whereas this annotation effort was solely targeted at explicit relations. For the cases where both annotators agreed on the connective's reading, a relation sense agreement of 82.1% (Cohen's Kappa of .79) was achieved. This corresponds to the third-level agreement of 70.4% (Cohen's Kappa of .74) for the PCC2.2 annotations, though again, note that here, this figure deals with explicit relations only.

2.5. Summary

This chapter provides an overview of the data and the connective lexicon that are used throughout this dissertation. As a contribution of this dissertation, the connectives and arguments layer of the PCC has been extended and additional data, sampled from Wikipedia and news articles, has been annotated from scratch, for connectives and their senses. In addition, DiMLex has been improved through several minor modifications. Parts of this chapter have been previously published in Bourgonje and Stede (2020b).

The data and the lexicon have been worked on to improve performance of the shallow discourse parser for German that is the ultimate practical purpose of this dissertation. Chapter 3 first explains the architecture of this parser, and subsequently, Chapters 4, 5, 6 and 7 zoom in on the individual components of the architecture.

Chapter 3

System Overview

In this chapter, we explain and discuss the pipeline architecture for end-to-end shallow discourse parsing that we adopt, followed by the technical details of the parser, which is open-source and made available online. As a practical contribution of this dissertation, the parser is meant to support end-to-end discourse parsing, where the input is plain text and the output are the discourse relations identified in this text, in a machine-readable format (JSON in our case). The pipeline architecture was introduced by Lin et al. (2014) and has been widely adopted since ((Kong et al., 2016; Laali et al., 2016; Li et al., 2016; Oepen et al., 2016; Stepanov and Riccardi, 2016; Wang and Lan, 2015, 2016), to cite a few).

Subsequently, the theoretical contributions of this dissertation are outlined in Chapters 4 to 7, focusing on individual sub-tasks of the shallow discourse parsing task. These chapters reflect both the sub-tasks themselves, and also their relative ordering in the processing pipeline.

3.1. Architecture

As explained in Section 1.3, shallow discourse parsing and the PDTB framework have basically become synonymous, and the way in which plain text is annotated manually (i.e., during the PDTB annotation campaigns) much resembles the way in which plain text is often annotated automatically (e.g., the pipeline architecture of Lin et al. (2014)).

In the PDTB annotation campaigns, from its first version (Prasad et al., 2006b) to its most recent third version (Webber et al., 2019), a distinction is made between Explicit and Implicit relations, the former referring to discourse relations with an explicit discourse connective and the latter comprising relations where no overt discourse connective is present (see Chapter 4 for more information and examples). Both types of relations have exactly two arguments (see Chapter 5 for more information and examples), and a particular relation sense assigned to them (see Chapter 6 for more information and examples). As explained in Chapter 2, the way that these components have been annotated, at least in the first two versions[1] of the PDTB, is by first spotting connectives and annotating their arguments and sense, thus establishing Explicit relations. Then, whenever two adjacent sentences in the same paragraph are not already linked by an Explicit relation, an Implicit relation between these sentences is posited and its sense is annotated.

This procedure is reflected by the first two steps in the pipeline architecture of Lin et al. (2014), which is illustrated in Figure 3.1, and which we adopt in this dissertation.

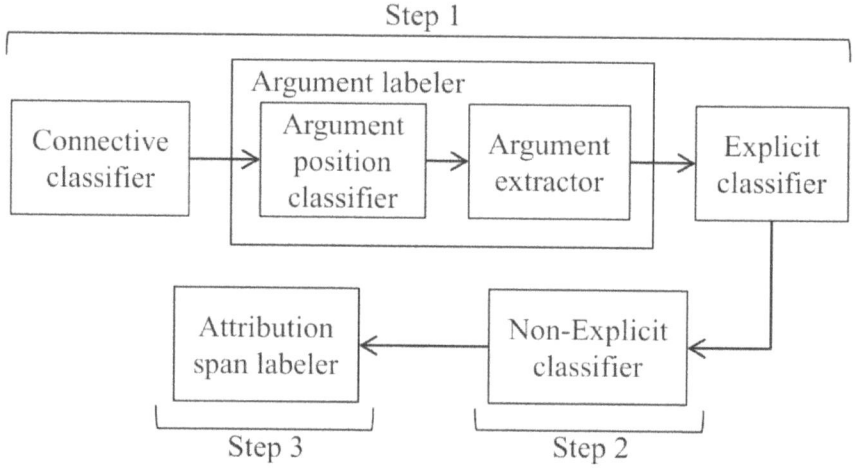

Figure 3.1: Lin et al. (2014, p.161) pipeline architecture

Note that we do not perform the third step of attribution labeling, since the PCC contains no annotations related to attribution. Attri-

---

[1]In the third version, intra-sentential Implicit relations are annotated as an extra step at the end.

bution labeling concerns the exclusion of certain phrases from the argument(s), as exemplified by (9) below, where the span attributing the belief that is held to Mr. Marcus ("Mr. Marcus believes") is excluded from the relation/its arguments.

(9) Mr. Marcus believes spot steel prices will continue to fall through early 1990 and then reverse themselves. (Example 14 from Prasad et al. (2006a, p.5))

In absence of specific attribution annotations in the PCC, this is excluded as a specific processing step, but implicitly included in the argument labeling sub-task. Equally excluded are `AltLex` and `EntRel` relations, on the basis of their low frequency in the PCC (only 122, 56 instances respectively, see Table 2.1)

Breaking down the end-to-end task in the sub-tasks of connective identification, argument labeling and sense classification has been demonstrated to achieve state-of-the-art results in the 2015 and 2016 CoNLL shared tasks on shallow discourse parsing (Xue et al., 2015, 2016). The modularity of the architecture allows focusing on individual sub-tasks, and evaluating them individually, as has been done in the shared task scoring setup. A known drawback of a pipeline architecture though is its susceptibility to error propagation. Incorrect classifications during connective identifications have negative impact on argument labeling, which in turn has negative impact on sense classification for explicit relations and the identification of implicit relations.

To the best of our knowledge, the only system for end-to-end discourse parsing that does not deploy a (modified version of this) pipeline architecture is described by Biran and McKeown (2015), who instead use a tagging-based approach and divide the task into processing intra-sentential and inter-sentential relations (as opposed to the more typical division into explicit and implicit relations). They apply two Conditional Random Field taggers and do introduce sequentiality in their parser by first looking for intra-sentential relations and then looking at adjacent sentences for inter-sentential relations. The second tagger, however, is not directly dependent on the results of the first one, and the system has fewer components in total (in fact, it only has two), thus reducing the impact of potential error propagation. Using this setup, they outperform Lin et al. (2014), reporting a final f1-score of 39.33, compared to 38.18 for Lin et al. (2014). This score has been improved upon by Oepen et al. (2016), who do use the pipeline architecture adopted from Lin et al. (2014), and the authors report an f1-score of 44.20. Note that this comparison has been made based on partial matching; i.e., a relation was considered to be correct if the connective (if present) was identified, each of the arguments share at least one noun and verb with the gold standard argument, and the relation type is correctly classified. Oepen et al. (2016) report an exact matching f1-score, where each token of the arguments has to match the gold standard version exactly, of 27.75.

In Chapters 5 to 7, both individual performance without error propagation (i.e., using gold standard information from upstream sub-tasks directly from the corpus annotations), and performance using the output of upstream sub-tasks is reported. As explained in Section 1.4, the focus in this dissertation is on explicit relations. To increase usability of the emerging end-to-end discourse parser however, we include a component for implicit relations as well. Due to a lack of sufficient annotations for other relation types (`AltLex`, `EntRel`, `NoRel`) in our German data, our parser ignores these additional PDTB relation types.

3.2. Technical Details

This section explains the technical details of the end-to-end shallow discourse parser implementation and motivates the design decisions. In order to run the parser on a server and allow clients to send input and receive output, the back-end of the parser is exposed through two endpoints via a Representational state transfer Application Programming Interface (REST-API) (Fielding, 2000). The first endpoint allows training the (individual components of the) parser, for which the PCC is used. The second endpoint, relying on a trained parser, takes plain text as input and extracts discourse relations from this text. These are then returned in a Javascript Object Notation (JSON) format, based on the format used in the 2016 CoNLL shared task on shallow discourse parsing (Xue et al., 2016), but slightly modified: the shared task JSON format consists of a text file, in which every line represents a JSON object, but crucially, the entire file is not a JSON object. We modified this by appending every output relation to a list, which is then dumped to one single JSON object, to allow easier parsing of the parser output for downstream tasks. Appendix

B illustrates the parser output, given the input shown in Appendix A.

Because of the extensive availability of NLP-related components and libraries (SciKit-learn, SpaCy, NLTK, PyTorch, etc.), the parser is implemented in the Python programming language, and is available[2] under a Creative Commons Attribution NonCommercial Share-Alike 4.0 International License[3].

The parser relies on the availability of a bert-serving server[4], which has to be started first. When this is up and running, the main method (`Parser.py`) of the parser can be started, and a Python Flask[5] application is started, exposing the two endpoints. To make installation more convenient, in addition, the file to build a Docker[6] container is provided. A Docker container is essentially a minimal version of the operating system with all the dependencies required for the service in question installed on it. The service itself is then run, and can be communicated with, over the specified port number. This has the advantage that installation is reduced to one or two simple commands, and the service can be executed without interfering with other system settings and libraries (such as Python libraries installed on the host system).

After either starting the Flask application by running `Parser.py` or building and starting the Docker container, the parser has to be trained. This takes ca. 2 minutes on a CPU/Laptop (6 cores, 2,20 GhZ, 24GB RAM). After training, plain text input can be parsed. Parsing the input file shown in Appendix A takes ca. 30 seconds (6.5 tokens/second).

Detailed instructions on how to install and use the parser are included in Appendix C.

---

[2]https://github.com/PeterBourgonje/GermanShallowDiscourseParser
[3]https://creativecommons.org/licenses/by-nc-sa/4.0/
[4]https://pypi.org/project/bert-serving-server/
[5]https://flask.palletsprojects.com
[6]https://www.docker.com

.

Chapter 4

Connective Identification

Signaling discourse relations can be done in various different ways. In the case of a text, the author can choose to express a relation through semantics, syntax, or lexical items. In (10), semantics is used and the antonymy between a bad mood and euphoria is enough to infer a contrastive relation between the two sentences.

(10) *I was prepared to be in a very bad mood tonight. Now, I feel maybe there's a little bit of euphoria.* (wsj_2169)

In other cases, the relation may be signaled by a particular word or phrase, such as in (11), where the phrase "Trouble is" signals a concessive relation.

(11) *Mr. Payson, an art dealer and collector, sold Vincent van Gogh's "Irises" at a Sotheby's auction in November 1987 to Australian businessman Alan Bond. Trouble is, Mr. Bond has yet to pay up, and until he does, Sotheby's has the painting under lock and key.* (wsj_2113)

Another way to signal discourse relations is through the use of a *(discourse) connective*, such as in (12), where the causal relation between the two segments can first and foremost be subscribed to the presence of "because".

(12) *The 11 banks in the syndicate sustained no monetary losses <u>because</u> none of the credit facility had been drawn down.* (wsj_2162)

Connectives play a central role in the PDTB, and whenever a relation is signaled by a connective, that relation is said to be *explicit*.
The clear-cut distinction between *explicit* and *implicit* relations in
the PDTB may lead the naive reader to believe that implicit relations
are just explicit relations without a connective, or that a connective
is only needed when the relation cannot be inferred from the semantics of the arguments alone. Though this may be the case for some
relations, examples (13) and (14) aptly demonstrate that this is not
necessarily the case.

(13) *Talks have broken off between Machinists representatives at
Lockheed Corp. and the Calabasas, Calif., aerospace company.
The union is continuing to work through its expired contract,
however.* (RST-DT, (Carlson et al., 2002))

(14) *Talks have broken off between Machinists representatives at
Lockheed Corp. and the Calabasas, Calif., aerospace company.
The union is continuing to work through its expired contract.*

The presence of "however" in (13) gives rise to a concessive reading.
When this connective is deleted, the reading changes and the relation
is more likely to be causal or additive and Sporleder and Lascarides
(2008) demonstrate that in an application scenario, treating implicit
relations like explicit relations without a connective is unlikely to be
successful.

Though considered to be a closed lexical class, connectives are
challenging to process and can be ambiguous in two different ways.
Consider examples (15) - (17).

(15) *He is now changing the place he sleeps every night, sometimes
more than once a night.* (wsj_2013)

(16) *Once it gets there, a company can do with it what it wishes.*
(wsj_0989)

(17) *Normally, once the underlying investment is suspended from
trading, the options on those investments also don't trade.*
(wsj_1962)

In (15), the word "once" is an adverb with *sentential* reading and
does not serve to relate any propositions in particular. Contrary to

(15), in (16), "once" is connecting the two propositions conveying a company arriving at some point, and this same company doing whatever it wishes with "it". In this case, "once" has *discourse* or *connective* reading. The difference between (15) and (16) with respect to "once" illustrates the first type of ambiguity, being the ambiguity on a functional level, i.e., the difference between sentential or discourse reading. Not all connectives display this type of ambiguity, and others such as *because, nevertheless* and *however* always signal a discourse relation, thus always have discourse reading.

In addition to this functional ambiguity (*sentential* vs. *discourse* reading), connectives can exhibit sense ambiguity. This second type of ambiguity is illustrated by (16) and (17). In (16), "once" signals a temporal relation between a company arriving at some point, and this company doing whatever it wishes. In (17) however, "once" signals a conditional relation between the ability to trade some underlying investments and the ability to trade options on these investments. Similarly to the functional ambiguity situation, not all connectives display this second type of ambiguity. Moreover, some connectives display both (like *once*), some always have discourse reading but can express different senses (such as *however*) and some can have either sentential or discourse reading, but only ever express one particular sense if they have discourse reading (*simultaneously*, for example).

This chapter deals with the processing of connectives with regard to their functional ambiguity (i.e., the difference between examples (15) and (16)). It explains the first component in the processing pipeline explained in Chapter 3, responsible for connective identification. In this chapter, we only deal with ambiguity on a functional level, and return to sense ambiguity later in Chapter 6. The key contribution of this chapter is the implementation of a connective identification component for German, based on contextualised embeddings and manually crafted syntactic features, combined with linguistic knowledge explicitly encoded in DiMLex, and we present the first general results for connective identification for German. Due to the central role connectives play in this dissertation, the following subsections first provide a discussion of connectives in the broader context of discourse markers. Subsequently, related work on connective identification is discussed and our approach to connective identification for German is explained and evaluated on the PCC and additional data annotated as another contribution of this dissertation. Parts of this chapter have been previously published in Bourgonje and Stede (2018a, 2020a).

4.1. Connectives & Discourse Markers

In the preceding text, the term *(discourse) connective* has been used to refer to explicit lexical signals marking a discourse relation. In the field of discourse processing, definitions and categorisations have not been uncontroversial and several different terms for these lexical items are in use. Schiffrin (1987) uses the term *discourse marker*, defining it as "(...) linguistic, paralinguistic, or non-verbal elements that signal relations between units of talk (...)" (Schiffrin, 1987, p.40). This term is discussed and refined by Redeker (1991), who in the same paper introduces the term *discourse operator*: "a word or phrase - for instance, a conjunction, adverbial, comment clause, interjection - that is uttered with the primary function of bringing to the listener's attention a particular kind of linkage of the upcoming utterance with the immediate discourse context" (Redeker, 1991, p.1168). Cohen (1984) uses the term *clue words* to refer to "words which serve to indicate overall structure - phrases that link individual propositions to form one coherent presentation" (Cohen, 1984, p.251). The term *cue phrase* is used by Grosz and Sidner (1986), and adopted by Knott and Dale (1994), who set out to construct a theory-independent list of cue phrases in a data-driven way, reconciling theoretical relation taxonomies with evidence from (academic) texts. They come up with a test to establish whether or not something can be considered a cue phrase, based on, among other things, whether or not the units it connects form a "mini-discourse" (Knott and Dale, 1994, p.17), or a proposition on their own. This condition is reflected by the more formal definition[1] of Pasch et al. (2003, p.331), who state that a lexical item **X** is a *connective*, when:

- **X** is not inflectable,

- **X** does not assign case to its syntactic environment,

- **X** expresses some specific, two-place semantic relation,

---

[1]More specifically the fourth requirement of the definition.

- the arguments of the relational meaning of **X** are propositional structures,

- the verbalizations of the arguments of the relational meaning of **X** can be clauses.

We adopt the definition from Pasch et al. (2003). However, following Stede (2002), we drop the second requirement, because we do include prepositions that have a discourse function. We adopt and translate[2] the term and use *connective* throughout this dissertation.

The set of connectives for a particular language is uncontroversially assumed to be syntactically heterogeneous and includes adverbials, subordinating and coordinating conjunctions. By virtue of dropping the second requirement of Pasch et al. (2003), we include prepositions as well. The PDTB2.0 guidelines only include subordinating and coordinating conjunctions and adverbials (Prasad et al., 2007, p.8), but in the PDTB3.0 guidelines, prepositions (that take clausal complements) have been included as well (Webber et al., 2019, p.7). An overview of markers, cue phrases and connectives is provided by Danlos et al. (2018), who use the umbrella term *Discourse Relational Devices* and first distinguish between discourse connectives on the one hand and discourse markers or particles on the other, where the former establish a two-place relation between abstract objects (Asher, 1993) (see also Chapter 5), whereas the latter establish a one-place relation. Typical examples of markers or particles are interjections such as *well, yeah* and *right*. The group of discourse connectives is further split into *primary* and *secondary* connectives. The operationalisation we use throughout this dissertation matches the definition of primary connectives from Danlos et al. (2018).

In addition to not (explicitly) defining the syntactic group(s) of connectives, the definition speaks of lexical items and says nothing about whether or not connectives are, or should be, single words or multi-word units. Indeed, the connectives listed in DiMLex (see 2) are a combination of single words and phrasal elements, where the latter can be either continuous (e.g., *as long as*) or discontinuous (e.g., *either ... or*). The challenges that both the syntactic heterogeneity and the surface form variations pose to the task of connective identification are described in the following sections, but first, Section

---

[2]Pasch et al. (2003) is a German book.

4.2 provides an overview of related work on the task of connective identification.

4.2. Related Work

Most work on (shallow) discourse parsing and its individual sub-tasks has been carried out on English. The PDTB3.0 contains ca. 53k annotated relations, compared to 2,208 annotated relations in the PCC. Basically, for any language other than English, the number of available annotations is comparatively low, as illustrated by Table 4.1, taken from Bourgonje and Schäfer (2019, p.107). For a discussion of related work on connective identification, we therefore mostly have to look for approaches that apply to English and more specifically, the PDTB.

Corpus name	Language	Annotation style	Tokens
RSTBT (Iruskieta et al., 2013)	Basque	RST	28,658
CDTB (Zhou and Xue, 2015)	Chinese	PDTB	63,239
SCTB (Cao et al., 2018)	Chinese	RST	11,067
NLDT (Redeker et al., 2012)	Dutch	RST	21,355
PDTB (Prasad et al., 2008)	English	PDTB	1,100,990
GUM (Zeldes, 2017)	English	RST	82,691
RSTDT (Carlson et al., 2002)	English	RST	184,158
STAC (Asher et al., 2016)	English	SDRT	41,666
ANNODIS (Afantenos et al., 2012)	French	SDRT	25,050
PCC (Stede and Neumann, 2014)	German	RST	29,883
RRST (Toldova et al., 2017)	Russian	RST	243,896
RSTSTB (da Cunha et al., 2011)	Spanish	RST	50,565
SCTB (Cao et al., 2018)	Spanish	RST	12,699
CSTN (Cardoso et al., 2011)	Brazilian Portuguese	RST	51,041

Table 4.1: Corpora annotated for discourse relations from various languages and frameworks

Early and influential work on automatic disambiguation of discourse connectives, or cue phrases, is presented by Marcu (2000), who essentially used a set of regular expressions to capture surface characteristics of connectives, on a corpus annotated for the purpose. Another approach that turned out to be highly influential is described by Pitler and Nenkova (2009). They propose a set of features based on syntax and use these to disambiguate between both sentential vs. discourse reading (or discourse vs. non-discourse reading), and between senses in the PDTB. Using the gold standard syntax trees from the Penn Treebank (Marcus et al., 1993), they use a Maximum Entropy classifier in combination with the following features:

- **self category** The highest node in the tree which dominates the words in the connective but nothing else. This corresponds to the part-of-speech tag for single word connectives, but for multi-word connectives is the label of the node they are in.

- **parent category** This is the parent of the (node of the) self category.

- **(left|right) sibling category** This is the category of the left or right sibling of the self category node, and is set to None if there is no left or right sibling.

- **right sibling contains a VP** Boolean feature for whether or not the right sibling (if it exists) contains a VP.

- **right sibling contains a trace** Boolean feature for whether or not the right sibling (if it exists) contains a trace (e.g., a sign of ellipsis).

With their best scoring setup, they report an f-score of 94.19 for the connective identification task.

In their pipeline architecture for end-to-end shallow discourse parsing, Lin et al. (2014) expand on the feature set of Pitler and Nenkova (2009) with the following:

- **surface-level bigrams** The left-neighbour and the current word, and the current word and the right-neighbour

- **part-of-speech bigrams** The part-of-speech of the left-neighbour and that of the current word, and the part-of-speech of the current word and that of the right-neighbour

- **path to the root node** The path from the current word to the root node of the constituency tree.

- **compressed path** A compressed version of the path to the root node, in which adjacent identical labels are deleted, e.g., NP-NP-VP-S becomes NP-VP-S.

Using this extended feature set and a Maximum Entropy classifier and gold standard syntax trees, they report an f-score of 95.36.

In the 2016 CoNLL shared task on shallow discourse parsing, the best-performing system (Li et al., 2016) for the sub-task of connective identification reports an f-score of 98.38. They use the features that are added by Lin et al. (2014) (but not those from Pitler and Nenkova (2009)) in combination with a Maximum Entropy classifier. The second-best system for this sub-task (Oepen et al., 2016) reports an f1-score of 91.79, using a combination of surface-level and part-of-speech tag n-grams, the Lin et al. (2014) features and the features used by the winning system of the preceding year (Wang and Lan, 2015), in combination with an SVM classifier.

Earlier work on German connectives is done by Dipper and Stede (2006), who use a subset of nine connectives and train the Brill tagger on distinguishing between sentential and discourse reading. They manually annotated 30k sentences from the TIGER corpus (Brants et al., 2004) for these nine connectives. On this subset, consisting of the connectives[3] *allein (only)*, *also (so/therefore)*, *auch (also)*, *dann (then)*, *doch (but/nevertheless)*, *ferner (further(more))*, *nur (only)*, *so (so)* and *sonst (otherwise)*, an f-score of 93.95 is reported.

To the best of our knowledge, we are the first to present performance for German connective identification without limiting ourselves to a particular subset of connective types.

4.3. Connectives in the Data

4.3.1. Connectives in the Potsdam Commentary Corpus

To train and evaluate our approach, we use the PCC in its 2.2 version (Bourgonje and Stede, 2020b). Recall from Chapter 2 that the PCC has 33,222 words in total and that there are 1,112 annotated explicit discourse relations, hence 1,112 connectives. For some of the experiments reported on in this chapter, we exploit the syntax annotation layer of the PCC, as this allows us to compare performance using gold standard parse trees to performance using automatically produced parse trees. For downstream tasks (i.e., argument extraction and sense classification) though, we continue with automatically

---

[3]Both uppercase and lowercase variants are included.

produced parse trees as this provides a more realistic estimate of performance in the end-to-end scenario, where plain text without any annotations is used as input.

The PCC contains 175 connective types. If we add the cases of sentential reading (e.g., cases like example (6) earlier in this chapter), we have a total of 2,669 instances to train and evaluate our approach on; 1,112 connective tokens and 1,557 non-connective tokens. Of the 175 connective types, 47 are singletons and only 66 occur more than 5 times, illustrating the rather long tail with low-frequency examples.

94 of the 175 connective types always have discourse reading in the PCC, meaning that, for these cases, the task of connective identification in theory could be handled by simple pattern matching (but our classifier has to learn them nonetheless, and so they are included in the training and test data). This group, however, only comprises 337 instances (13% of all data). Among the other 87%, distribution is heavily skewed. Connectives like *Und*[4] (*and*), *sondern* (*but/rather*) and *wenn* (*if*) have a high connective ratio, of 0.95, 0.93 and 0.97, respectively. On the other hand, connectives like *als* (*as*), *Wie* (*(such) as*) and *durch* (*through/by*) very seldom have connective reading, with a ratio of 0.08, 0.05 and 0.06, respectively.

In terms of surface form, the majority of connectives in the PCC are single words; there are 140 single word connective types (all tokens belonging to these 140 types make up 96% of all data), vs. 35 phrasal connective types (4% of all data). Of these 35 phrasal types, 17 are discontinuous (2% of all data).

4.3.2. Wikipedia & News Data

Section 2.4 explained the procedure of sampling and annotating additional data from Wikipedia and from news articles (henceforth: WN) . In this chapter, we use this data for the connective identification task. The sample from these two sources contains 75,587 words in total, with 940 connectives and 2,184 non-connective instances. The number of connectives here is considerably lower than in the PCC (especially the relative amount), because only the connectives of interest were annotated. This means that there probably are more connectives in the texts, in the surrounding 7 sentences (5 before, 2 after the connective of interest). For our experiments, we only use instances

---

[4]Note that we make a distinction between upper- and lower-case here.

which were confirmed, by the annotator, to be either a connective or not a connective.

Due to targeted sampling, the number of connective types (210) is higher than in the PCC. Of these, 78 always have discourse reading, making up 9% of all data. 171 connective types in this data are single words (94% of all data), vs. 39 that are phrasal (6% of all data). Of the 39 phrasal types, 10 are discontinuous (1% of all data).

Table 4.2 sums up the key characteristics of the two data sets used in this chapter.

	PCC	WN
number of words	33,222	75,587
connective tokens	1,112	940
non-connective tokens	1,557	2,184
connective types	175	210

Table 4.2: Key characteristics of the PCC and WN data

4.4. Identifying Connectives

Because the identification of connectives is the first component in our pipeline architecture, improving performance for this component is effort well-invested as it decreases the propagation of errors down the pipeline. Sections 4.4.1 to 4.4.3 explain how a baseline system based on contextualised embeddings is combined with information from DiMLex and with syntactic information. These setups are evaluated on the PCC and the WN data explained in Sections 4.3.1 and 4.3.2.

4.4.1. Contextualised Embeddings for Connective Identification

In recent years, traditional word-embeddings (Mikolov et al., 2013), attempting to represent the semantics of individual words, have moved on to include the context of these words to semantically represent longer sequences of tokens. In addition, these architectures allow pre-training on enormous amounts of data, and fine-tuning to particular tasks (Devlin et al., 2019; Peters et al., 2018; Radford et al., 2019). While this has been demonstrated to work on a number of benchmark

NLP tasks, these benchmark tasks still have considerably more train-ing data available than our German connective identification setup. For example, Devlin et al. (2019) fine-tune on 100k question-answer pairs from Rajpurkar et al. (2018) and 113k sentence pair completion examples from Zellers et al. (2018). In contrast, we only have 1,108 explicit relations in the PCC. We thus first establish a baseline using the Bidirectional Encoder Representations from Transformers (hence-forth: BERT) from Devlin et al. (2019) to see how well this system copes with the significantly smaller number of fine-tuning training samples.

This baseline setup uses all the connectives in the PCC as seeds. Whenever a seed (i.e., potential connective) is encountered in the text, we extract the entire sentence the candidate connective appears in. If the candidate is sentence-initial, we take its previous sentence as well. For this textual input, we retrieve the BERT embedding. This is then concatenated with the candidate's single-word embed-ding. The reason for including the isolated embedding separately is to differentiate between candidates appearing in the same sentence. Consider example (18), where "and" has sentential reading and "once" has discourse reading.

(18) But traders took profits and focused on crude oil inventories once that factor was eliminated. (wsj_1932)

Including the candidate separately prevents feeding the classifier two identical samples with different labels. Since we use the base version of a German BERT model,[5] this returns a 2304-dimensional vector.[6] This is then fed as input to a MultiLayer Perceptron classifier (all (hyper)parameter values set at their defaults[7]). We opt for a Mul-tiLayer Perceptron because of good results in earlier, related work (Bai and Zhao, 2018; Ostendorff et al., 2019; Pacheco et al., 2016). The results for the baseline are included in Table 4.3 in the rows re-lating to **BERT**. For the PCC, all scores in Table 4.3 are the result of 10-fold cross-validation (using weighted average of precision, recall and f1-score over all 10 runs). For the WN setup, training is done

---

[5]https://deepset.ai/german-bert

[6]The first 786 positions are set to a default if the candidate is not sentence-initial.

[7]https://scikit-learn.org/stable/modules/generated/sklearn.neural_network.MLPClassifier.html

on the PCC and evaluation on the WN data, illustrating the impact of domain transfer (i.e., training on the news commentary articles of the PCC, testing on the news and encyclopedia articles of the WN data).

4.4.2. Exploiting DiMLex for Connective Identification

A first attempt to improve over this (**BERT + DiMLex (seeds only)**) is essentially the same as the former setup, but instead of using all connectives in the PCC as seeds, we now use all entries (plus their orthographical variants) of DiMLex as seeds. With the connectives in DiMLex being a superset of those in the PCC, in the PCC setup, this effectively only adds negative examples to the data. The main motivation for using all DiMLex entries as the seed list is that for other corpora, connective candidates not appearing in the PCC will also be considered for connective identification.

Since information on whether or not a particular connective can have sentential reading is available in DiMLex, we exploit this information (and refer to it as **BERT + DiMLex ambiguity info**) by simply overruling the classifier prediction, as a post-processing step, in case it predicts a sentential reading when this does not correspond to its relevant DiMLex attribute. In addition, this setup assigns discourse reading for the relevant seeds from DiMLex, also if the candidate did not appear in the training data.

4.4.3. Including Syntactic Information for Connective Identification

As discussed in Section 4.2, Pitler and Nenkova (2009) started a tradition of disambiguating connectives based on a number of syntactic features. In earlier work (Bourgonje and Stede, 2018a), we adopt this strategy and use a combination of surface features and syntactic features for the binary classification of connectives (i.e., discourse vs. sentential reading). To further improve over our BERT baseline, we combine this syntactic information with the setup using BERT and also DiMLex. The syntactic information consists of the feature set from Lin et al. (2014), which in turn is based on, but expands the feature set proposed by Pitler and Nenkova (2009) (see Section 4.2). To obtain the constituency trees, we use the NLTK implementation of the Stanford Parser for German (Rafferty and Manning, 2008) and we use the Random Forect classifier from Pedregosa et al. (2011), following Bourgonje and Stede (2018a).

Since we have less training data available for German (both Pitler and Nenkova (2009) and Lin et al. (2014) work on English), we add some features that we expect to make certain patterns more explicit and easier to pick up on by the classifier. The information conveyed by these additional features is, in most cases, encoded in the Lin et al. (2014) set of features, but in a more implicit way. First, we add a feature indicating the main syntactic group of the connective to explicitly differentiate for the following five cases; prepositions, co-ordinating conjunctions, sub-ordinating conjunctions, adverbials and a label reserved for other cases[8]. Given enough training instances, this information is likely to surface from the part-of-speech, but we found it improved performance in our case. In addition, we add a binary feature that indicates whether or not the token is initial to a clause that starts with S or S-bar. While this would similarly surface through the part-of-speech bigrams for those tokens that are sentence-initial (but not necessarily for those that are S-bar initial), we found that making this explicit improved performance. Together, these two features improve the f1-score by about 2 points in earlier experiments (Bourgonje and Stede, 2018a). Finally, we add a feature specifying sentence length. The idea behind this feature is that as sentences get longer, the need for explicit structuring of the discourse increases, which would result in an increased probability of a candidate being a connective in longer sentences. However, to avoid sparsity in feature values, instead of using actual sentence length, we use six categories for this value; between 1 and 5 words, between 6 and 10 words, between 11 and 15 words, between 16 and 20 words, between 20 and 25 words and longer than 25 words.

We combine the information from BERT and the syntactic features explained above, dubbed **BERT + DiMLex + Syntactic features** in Table 4.3, by averaging the predictions from the Multi-Layer Perceptron from our BERT baseline and the RandForest classifier from Bourgonje and Stede (2018a). After this, the same post-processing as in **BERT + DiMLex ambiguity info** is applied.

49

		PCC	**WN**
BERT	precision	81.78	75.56
	recall	81.62	62.25
	f1-score	81.53	62.81
BERT + DiMLex (seeds only)	precision	86.24	81.63
	recall	86.11	62.33
	f1-score	86.14	67.55
BERT + DiMLex ambiguity info	precision	86.64	81.60
	recall	86.40	62.80
	f1-score	86.33	67.96
BERT + DiMLex + Syntactic features	precision	**87.75**	**81.87**
	recall	**87.59**	**66.73**
	f1-score	**87.57**	**71.12**

Table 4.3: Results combining embeddings, DiMLex and syntactic features. Note that due to weighted averaging, f1-score is not necessarily between precision and recal.

4.5. Results & Evaluation

A simple majority vote procedure (assigning the most frequent label for any given connective token) achieves an f1-score of 79.60 on the PCC. Just using BERT, without any (explicit) syntactic information, improves over this by about 1.9 points. A considerable improvement in performance is observed when we include the entries from DiMLex as seed list. However, as explained in Section 4.4.2, since the connectives in DiMLex are a superset of those in the PCC, this only adds negative examples to the data. The fact that performance improves on the PCC can thus be interpreted as an artefact of the data. For the WN setup however, in which it crucially does not only add negative samples, we equally see this jump in performance, from 62.81 to 67.55. Including post-processing, which overrides predictions not aligning with DiMLex, results in small improvements for both the PCC and the WN data. However, in both setups, this improvement is not statistically significant (p>0.02). Finally, adding syntactic information further improves performance for the PCC by about 1.2 points to a final f1-score of 87.57 for connective identification in the PCC. In the WN setup, we obtain a final f1-score of 71.12. This demonstrates that for connective identification, with the low number of training in-

---

[8]Like the discontinuous 'um...zu' (*in order...to*).

stances we have available for German, large-scale embeddings-based approaches can be augmented with external knowledge encoded into lexicons, as well as manually crafted and syntactically inspired features to improve performance. The drop in performance when going from the PCC to the WN data provides an estimate of performance loss when transferring from the news commentary domain the PCC to a different domain (in this case two domains put together; encyclopedia articles and news).

Since the setups relying on syntactic features obviously rely on the quality of the parse trees, parsing errors are one source of error. Table 1 from Bourgonje and Stede (2018a, p.330) illustrates that the difference between using gold standard and automatically produced parse trees is considerable, with ca. 4 points difference in f1-score. Particularly, with the way hyphens surrounded by whitespace are used in the PCC, treating them as sentence segmentation symbols would often make more sense, such as in example (19). The parser however, typically does not treat the hyphen (separated by whitespace) as a sentence segmentation symbol.

(19) Der Euro kommt - schon bald. (maz-4181)
     The euro is coming - and it's coming fast.

With regard to false positives, a frequent source of error were elided conjunction cases, both on NP and on VP level, where, possibly due to the omission, the plain conjunction construction was not properly recognised. This was obviously only the case for connectives belonging to the syntactic category of conjunctions, and NP examles are "die Seeburger oder Groß-Glienicker Mitspieler" (*the Seeburger or Groß-Glienicker contenders*), "spektakuläre, aber routinierte Einsatz" (*spectacular, but routine-like deployment*) and "Rad- und Skatewege" (*cycling and skating roads*). A VP example is included in (20), where the subject "Die Kinder" (*the kids*) is elided in the second part of the phrase, after "und" (*and*), and "und" here was incorrectly classified as a connective.

(20) Die Kinder aber werden älter und kosten immer mehr. (maz-16590)
     The kids are getting older and ever-more expensive.

With regard to false negatives, a frequent source of error was the presence of a comma before the connective. Again, this only happened for conjunction-type connectives, and an example is included in (21), in which the connective "und" (*and*) is incorrectly classified as having sentential reading.

(21) Zusatzangebote müssen her, und was bietet sich da in der grü-nen Waldstadt mehr an als die Beschäftigung mit der Natur? (maz-8727)
Additional offers are needed, and what better to propose in a city in such a forested area than being in and around the forest?

Particularly for "und", the preceding comma seems to be a rela-tively reliable predictor and in the PCC, in 18 out of the 20 cases where *und* is preceded by a comma, it serves as a connective. Due to the frequency of the comma in general, in combination with the low number of training samples, this is probably not something that the classifier is able to reliably learn from the data.

Section 4.2 lists performance for the connective identification task for English. Though not implemented in combination with BERT and a connective lexicon, in earlier experiments we iteratively down-sampled the amount of (English) training data from the PDTB and demonstrated that when using syntactic information only, perfor-mance for German is on par with performance for English (Bour-gonje and Stede, 2018a, p.330). Based on the results presented here, we expect the proposed procedure, particularly the exploiting of a connective lexicon, to be beneficial for performance on connective identification in English as well.

4.6. Summary

In conclusion, this chapter provided our definition of connectives and discussed alternative definitions. We described the key characteristics of the Potsdam Commentary Corpus and the Wikipedia and news ar-ticles with regard to connective frequencies. The main contribution of this chapter is the introduction of the first complete results for Ger-man connective identification (earlier studies focused on a subset of connectives only). We combined a contextualised embeddings-based approach with linguistic knowledge encoded in a connective lexicon and syntactic features and demonstrated a performance improvement when doing so. Our method is trained and evaluated on the PCC. In order to establish domain influence, and to demonstrate that specifically the inclusion of DiMLex can counter-act domain influence, we evaluate our method on Wikipedia and news data specifically annotated for the purpose. Parts of this chapter are taken from work that has been published earlier (Bourgonje and Stede, 2018a, 2020a).

The connective classifier described in this chapter is the first component in the pipeline for end-to-end shallow discourse parsing. In Chapter 5, the next component in the pipeline, that of argument extraction, is discussed.

Chapter 5

Argument Extraction

In Chapter 4, discourse relations were uncovered by identifying and disambiguating lexical cues, i.e., the discourse connectives. The third criterion in the Pasch et al. (2003) definition mentions a two-place semantic relation, and the fourth and fifth hint at what these two elements are, i.e., *propositional structures* and items of which the relational meaning can be verbalised as a clause. This definition remains rather vague about what this looks like in practice. In addition, since the criteria serve to define a connective, they do not say anything about arguments for non-explicit relations.

In the PDTB, the definition of arguments relies on that of *Abstract Objects* (Asher, 1993) and is furthermore annotated according to the Minimality Principle, according to which "only as many clauses and/or sentences should be included in an argument selection as are minimally required and sufficient for the interpretation of the relation." (Prasad et al., 2007, p.14). Arguments typically include full and finite clauses, but can also be larger, e.g., multiple sentences, or smaller, e.g., VPs, nominalised constructions (hence NPs) or discourse deictics (*this, that*). The addition of intra-sentential implicit relations in the PDTB3.0 (Prasad et al., 2019) means the addition of more sub-clausal units as arguments, at least for implicit relations.

The annotation of PDTB relations typically occurs in a process similar to the pipeline architecture explained in Chapter 3. In the PDTB Annotator (Lee et al., 2016), an annotator first selects a connective span and its two argument spans, and subsequently other relations are added. By contrast, in RST analyses, the segmentation of text plays a much more central role, through the recognition of *El-*

ementary Discourse Units (EDUs), which is a first step for any RST annotation (manual or automatic). EDUs similarly lack a detailed, formal definition, and are defined as "units (...) of any size from typical lexical items to entire paragraphs or larger" (Mann et al., 1989, p.16), with the addition that units are generally considered to be "roughly clauses, except that clausal subjects and objects and restrictive relative clauses are considered parts of their host clauses rather than separate units." (Mann et al., 1989, p.16).

An attempt to both operationalise and unify the segmentation procedures among different theories for discourse representation is described in Zeldes et al. (2019). For the purpose of this work, we adopt the PDTB2.0 definition of an argument. This means that for explicit relations, the minimally required text span that is needed to interpret the relation is annotated (see Stede (2015) for more details). For implicit relations, in line with the PDTB2.0, adjacent sentences that are not already connected by an explicit relation are annotated. Thus, for explicit relations, arguments can be (sub-)clausal, single or multiple sentences, while for implicit relations, arguments are always sentences in the traditional, orthographic sense (i.e., starting with an upper-cased word, and ending on a period, question mark or exclamation mark, for example). This effectively renders the argument extraction task for implicit relations a simple case of sentence segmentation. In our final processing pipeline, we thus assign a relation sense to adjacent sentences not already involved in an explicit (or `AltLex`) relation, without considering argument spans in more detail. For explicit relations, a more sophisticated procedure is required.

The main contribution of this chapter is the definition of a set of heuristics based on sentential syntax (experimenting with both constituency and dependency trees) to extract the exact spans that make up both arguments for explicit relations. The following subsections provide an overview of related work, explain the characteristics of arguments of discourse relations in the PCC, and provide the details of our approach and discuss its performance on the PCC. The content of this chapter is based on previously published work (Bourgonje and Stede, 2019).

5.1. Related Work

For related work on this sub-task of discourse parsing, we have to look at work on English, as to the best of our knowledge, no comparable approaches working on German exist. The 2015 and 2016 CoNLL shared tasks on Shallow Discourse Parsing (Xue et al., 2015, 2016) reported scores on the argument extraction sub-task, and for this particular task, Oepen et al. (2016) report f1-scores of 52.0 and 76.2 for external and internal arguments, respectively. The figures for Lin et al. (2014) are 47.7 and 70.3. Wang and Lan (2015) report the best scores, with 50.7 and 77.4. All three systems use a pipeline architecture and work on the end-to-end task.

Specifically focusing on the extraction of discourse arguments, Wellner and Pustejovsky (2007) approach the issue by locating the lexical head of the argument in a dependency tree structure, side-stepping issues with discourse segmentation (which can to some extent be relatively arbitrary, for example with respect to whether or not to include unit-initial or unit-final punctuation marks). They report accuracy figures of 69.8 for external arguments and 90.8 for internal arguments in their best-scoring setup. Baldridge and Elwell (2008) use the same approach and improve upon it by deploying specialized rankers for individual connectives or connectives grouped by syntactic type (as, for example, adverbials tend to have their arguments further away than conjunctions), boosting accuracy for both arguments by 9%. Due to the smaller size of training data available for German, we decided against experimenting with this setup, expecting the drawbacks of data sparsity to be too severe. Additionally, we would like to point out that while Wellner and Pustejovsky (2007) scores arguments based on lexical head matching, we use precision and recall for all tokens that make up the arguments, and so therefore the scores cannot directly be compared. More recently, an LSTM-based approach without any manual input (in the form of hand-crafted rules) is explored in Hooda and Kosseim (2017). While promising, their performance relies on the availability of training data and, for the English scenario, does not improve on earlier work.

Since the PDTB is annotated over the same text as the Penn TreeBank, gold standard syntax trees are available, making it possible to investigate alignment of discourse arguments with syntactic boundaries. Dines et al. (2005) do exactly this, and find that a major source of lack of alignment is attribution (to someone other than the author of the text, usually a quote attributed to some speaker). While we acknowledge the impact of attribution on discourse segmentation, in the Potsdam Commentary Corpus we do not encounter any non-adjacent relation arguments where the intervening material is due to attribution.

5.2. Arguments of Explicit Relations in the Potsdam Commentary Corpus

Every discourse relation we consider contains exactly two arguments. In PDTB vocabulary, these are referred to as *Arg1* and *Arg2*. This refers to the unmarked textual order of both arguments. Cases where *Arg2* precedes *Arg1* in the text, such as in (22), make up a small minority[1]. In (22), *Arg1* is in italics, the connective underlined and *Arg2* in bold face.

(22) <u>When</u> **Maj. Moises Giroldi, the leader of the abortive coup in Panama, was buried**, *his body bore several gunshot wounds, a cracked skull and broken legs and ribs.* (wsj_2013)

A more formal definition then, is that *Arg2* is the argument the connective is syntactically integrated with. *Arg1* is simply the other argument. In the absence of a connective, for implicit relations, *Arg1* is simply the first and *Arg2* the second sentence of any given sentence pair[2]. We adopt this scheme, but, following Stede and Neumann (2014), change the naming convention throughout this dissertation, and when not referring to PDTB data, consistently refer to *Arg2* as *intarg* (for internal argument) and to *Arg1* as *extarg* (for external argument).

An example is illustrated in (23), where again the *extarg* is in italics, the connective underlined and the *intarg* in bold face[3].

(23) Und FDP-Luftikus Jürgen W. Möllemann bereist seinerseits schon jetzt eifrig den Nahen Osten, um *für diesen Fall gerüstet*

---

[1]Approximately 4% of all relations in the PDTB2.0.

[2]This does not hold anymore for the PDTB3.0 (see Webber et al. (2019, p.12) for details), but we use the PDBT2 scheme.

[3]Note that this text snippet contains two more connectives (*Und* and *um...zu*), which are not marked here.

zu sein <u>und</u> **sich als neuer liberaler Außenminister zu empfehlen.** (maz-6539)
And FDP-member Jürgen W. Mölleman is eagerly visiting the Near East regions, to prepare himself for this issue and to suggest himself as a new liberal foreign minister.

In the example, both arguments are considerably shorter than the sentence (both are VP nodes in the PCC gold standard syntax). Tables 5.1 and 5.2 display the most frequent syntactic labels for argument for all relations in the PCC, based on the gold standard syntax trees. The labels are based on the TIGER scheme (Brants et al., 2002), where S, VP, CS, NP and CVP, respectively, indicate a sentence, verb phrase, coordinated sentence, noun phrase and coordinated verb phrase. If some argument did not exactly match all leaves under a particular node in the tree, we extracted the first parent to all tokens of the argument and took its label. The percentage in parenthesis is the fraction of cases that were exactly matching the node label. For example, for *intargs*, for 75% of all cases grouped under S, the token span exactly matched all leaves under the S node.

Argument Label	Relative Frequency
S	**67%** (75%)
VP	**8%** (17%)
CS	**7%** (14%)
NP	**6%** (10%)
CVP	**4%** (2%)
others	**8%** (25%)

Table 5.1: *intarg shapes in the PCC*

Argument Label	Relative Frequency
S	**74%** (45%)
CS	**8%** (18%)
multiple sentences	**6%** (0%)
NP	**4%** (10%)
VP	**3%** (6%)
others	**5%** (12%)

Table 5.2: *extarg shapes in the PCC*

Despite the lack of a formal, syntactic definition, we see that in the majority of cases, the argument span resembles the syntactic definition of a sentence, though for *extargs* it exactly matches an S node in only 45% of cases. Considering the less frequent types and their internal distribution, the picture becomes a bit more fuzzy. For *intargs*, if the gold standard token span most closely resembles a VP, it exactly matches all leaves of that VP in only 17% of cases. And despite the requirement of arguments to express some proposition (where arguably a verb has to be included), 6% of *intargs* and 4% of *extargs* most closely resemble an NP, where for both argument types, in 90% of cases the exact token span was even smaller than the NP node.

Though the argument spans often do not exactly match all tokens under a particular node, the numbers in Tables 5.1 and 5.2 (and particularly the fact that the S node is by far the most frequent one for both argument types) suggest that syntax may help in extracting argument spans. In this chapter, we explore to what extent it does, by constructing a set of heuristics based on syntactic information to identify the exact token spans that make up the arguments.

5.3. Syntax-inspired Heuristics to Extract Explicit Relation Arguments

As mentioned in Section 5.2, the *intarg* is the argument the connective is syntactically integrated with, and the *extarg* then is the other argument. Given our syntax-inspired approach, this calls for a different approach for both argument types, which is reflected by the structure of the remainder of this section, with Section 5.3.1 focusing on *intargs* and Section 5.3.2 focusing on *extargs*. Results are reported for both types, first assuming gold standard connective annotations, then using predictions from a connective classifier as described in Chapter 4.

5.3.1. *Intargs*

A major cue in the extraction of the token span that makes up the *intarg* is both the position and the syntactic type of the connective. As a baseline, we extract all tokens from the sentence the connective appears in, excluding the connective itself.[4]. Both for the baseline and

---

[4]Whether or not the connective token(s) should be included in the *intarg* is essentially an arbitrary decision, the PCC annotation guidelines state they should be excluded.

for attempts to improve on it, we make an important design decision (and also a limiting factor) by only considering single sentences when extracting tokens for the argument. That is, we do not consider the possibility of arguments spanning over multiple sentences. This is the case in 2% of *intargs*. An example of this baseline, with *intarg* tokens in bold face, is included in example (24):

(24) <u>Doch</u> **unterm Strich stehen Brandenburgs Schulen ganz gut da.** (maz-00002)
But all in all, Brandenburg's schools are doing quite well.

The first attempt to improve over this baseline consists of an approach based on heuristics for dependency trees. The dependency trees for the input sentences are generated using the German model from spaCy[5], which is trained on the TIGER (Brants et al., 2004) and WikiNER (Nothman et al., 2013) corpora. We locate the connective in the dependency tree and recursively extract all the tokens under the head of the connective token. In case of multi-token connectives, we take the first token for this procedure[6]. After that, we apply a set of rules resulting from error analysis on earlier iterations of the output. First of all, similar to the baseline, we exclude the connective token(s) from the *intarg* token span. Next we include sentence-final punctuation, as this is typically not under the head of the connective token in the dependency tree, but is part of *intarg* according to the annotation guidelines[7] (Stede, 2015). Finally, if the connective is a conjunction, we only take all tokens that, in the plain text, are to the right of the connective.

A second attempt to improve over the baseline is based on constituency trees and heuristics around them. These trees are obtained using the NLTK (Bird and Loper, 2004) implementation of the Stanford parser with the German Probabilistic Context Free Grammar (PCFG) model (Rafferty and Manning, 2008). We locate the connective in the constituency tree, find the first parent node that is an S, CS or VP, and extract all tokens of this sub-tree. Then we again exclude the connective token(s) from this token list, and similar to the dependency approach, take only tokens that are to the right of

---

[5]https://spacy.io/models/de
[6]7% of all explicit relations in the PCC have a multi-token connective.
[7]Though not always consistently annotated, see Section 5.3.1.1

the connective if it is a conjunction (or any tokens in between the connective tokens in case of discontinuous connectives).

The precision, recall and f1-scores are calculated based on token overlap of the actual and the predicted argument. Every token that is predicted to be in the *intarg* of a particular relation and actually is in the *intarg* of that relation adds to the true positives. Every token that is predicted to be in the *intarg*, but actually is not, adds to the false positives, and every token that is predicted not to be in the *intarg*, but actually is, adds to the false negatives. The same procedure is used for *extargs*. For example, suppose that of the actual *extarg* "für diesen Fall gerüstet zu sein" from example (23), only the token span "für diesen Fall" was extracted as *extarg* by our method. This would result in 3 true positives and 3 false negatives. In the end, all true positives, false positives and false negatives are used to calculate precision, recall, and subsequently f1-score. In related work, alternative scoring methods are used, such as by Wellner and Pustejovsky (2007), who use lexical head matching, or Xue et al. (2016), who only count an argument as correct if it exactly matches the actual token span (partial matching is given no credit in the final scoring, but is reported on by the scorer used in the shared task). While these scoring methods provide an accurate picture of performance for the shallow discourse parsing task itself, we argue that the token-based metric we use provides a better indication of performance for downstream tasks that use discourse relations as input. Lexical head matching may provide an inaccurate picture in the case such downstream tasks are relying on what else is extracted (other than the lexical head of the argument), and the exact matching of Xue et al. (2016) may be too harsh in the sense that downstream applications can also work with partial matches and do not require an exact match of the argument span. All numbers reported on in this chapter are based on our token-based metric, and are the result of 10-fold cross-validation in combination with micro-averaging.

The results for the baseline, dependency- and constituency-based approaches are included in Table 5.3. These scores are obtained when using the actual, gold standard connectives. In the pipeline architecture implementation, only the constituency-based approach is implemented. The difference between the two approaches is small and since the connective classification component exploits information from the constituency tree, this tree can be re-used for argument extraction,

	Precision	Recall	F1-score
Baseline	56.49	94.51	70.85
Dependency trees	84.93	83.14	84.03
Constituency trees	**87.22**	**81.67**	**84.35**

Table 5.3: Results for intarg extraction

whereas using the dependency-approach would require another parsing step. This is why only the constituency-based approach is implemented in the pipeline architecture. When using predicted connectives (as opposed to gold standard connectives), we can therefore only present results for the constituency-based approach, for which we report a precision, recall and f1-score, respectively, of 90.30, 62.25 and 73.69. Both the false positives and false negatives from the connective classifier thus result in a 11-point drop in f1-score for *intarg* extraction, illustrating the impact of error propagation. In comparison, Oepen et al. (2016) report a difference of under 3 points for *intarg* extraction, with an f1-score for their connective classification component of 94.4 (compared to our 87.57).

5.3.1.1. Results & Evaluation

In the setup using gold standard connectives, both approaches improve over the baseline by over 13 points in f1-score. They perform very much comparable to each other. After error analysis, we found that for the dependency approach, a common source of parsing errors was "aber" (*but/however*) as a connective, such as in examples (25) and (26), where the dependents of the connective were only "Die" (25) and "in erster Linie" (26), resulting in these segments to become *intargs*, instead of the correct entire sentence (25) or second half of the sentence (26). Another frequent cause of error were cases where the approach of selecting all dependents of the head of the connective does not suffice, as is the case for "auch" (*also*) in example (27). Here, this procedure extracts "eine Hemmschwelle" only, instead of the entire sentence.

(25) Die aber scheint nur bei zwei Standorten an der Berliner Straße garantiert: (maz-6165)
However, this seems to be guaranteed only at two locations on the Berliner street:

(26) Zu danken ist das Projekt vielen, in erster Linie aber der Eigenini-
tiative der Dorfbewohner. (maz-16353)
*Much is thanks to the project, but first and foremost to the ini-
tiative of the villagers.*

(27) Mit der PR-Aktion wurde eben auch eine Hemmschwelle über-
wunden. (maz-16360)
*With the PR campaign, an inhibition threshold was also over-
come.*

Furthermore, we found that sometimes punctuation marks were
ignored by the dependency parser, but taken as cues by the annotator,
as in example (28), where the dependency approach extracted (for
the connective "und" (*and*)) the complete phrase "wissen theoretisch
Bescheid - in der Realität aber enden leider zu viele Fahrten aus den
genannten Gründen verhängnisvoll.", whereas the annotator selected
only "wissen theoretisch Bescheid -". Because accommodating to this
tends to overfitting on the domain and data set, we decided against
implementing an extra rule for these cases.

(28) Sicher, wir haben das alles schon gehört und wissen theoretisch
Bescheid - in der Realität aber enden leider zu viele Fahrten aus
den genannten Gründen verhängnisvoll. (maz-5873)
*Sure, we've heard all this before and theoretically know all about
it - but in reality too many trips end fatally for the reasons
mentioned.*

For the constituency based approach, we also ran into the issue
with punctuation that we mentioned previously, where in particular
the hyphen is often used in the PCC to introduce some kind of related
material which is not picked up on by the parser (e.g., interpreting the
hyphen as a sentence segmentation symbol and whatever is following
it as an S-like structure would increase the accuracy, but of course
would need domain-specific parser training). This issue sometimes
led to incorrectly including intervening material (which the annotator left out), or looking for the higher S-node and including the
surrounding material as well (which the annotator deemed irrelevant
for the relation).

Another issue that emerged from error analysis had to do with in-
consistency in sentence-final punctuation annotation. Sentence-final

punctuation should be included according to the annotation guidelines, but is sometimes excluded; the tool that was used for annotation automatically suggests a piece of text as an argument, but if this automatic suggestion was incorrect, the annotators had to manually select the relevant piece of text in the GUI, where initial or final punctuation characters are easily overlooked. Because this is something that can easily be ignored during evaluation (i.e., ignoring any true positives, false positives or false negatives that match the regular expression for a punctuation symbol), we re-evaluated the scores, ignoring punctuation altogether, and found that this increased the f1-score by 0.35 points.

5.3.2. *Extargs*

Contrary to the *intarg* scenario, where we start with the position of the connective, in the *extarg* scenario, the relative position of the *extarg* has to be determined first (i.e., preceding the connective, as in example (29) or succeeding the connective, as in example (30)).

(29) *Die Stadt kann nur bedingt helfen,* <u>aber</u> **sie muss es endlich tun.** (maz-18914)
The city can only help to a limited extent, but it must finally do so.

(30) **Die Entlastungsstraße für Lkw führt** <u>zwar</u> **um die Altstadt herum,** *doch eine autofreie Stadt wird es nicht geben.* (maz-1679)
Although the bypass road for trucks runs around the old town, there will not be a car-free city.

(31) *Das Land hat künftig zu wenig Arbeit für zu viele Pädagogen.* <u>Und</u> **die Zeit drängt.** (maz-00001)
The country will have too little work for too many educators in the future. And time is running out.

Once located, if the *extarg* is in another sentence than the connective, as in example (31), there is little in terms of anchoring in cases where the *extarg* is not the entire sentence[8]. The distribution of *extarg*

---

[8]Though *extargs* are sentential more often than *intargs*, i.e., 74% vs. 67%, respectively (see Tables 5.1 and 5.2).

Relative position	Relative frequency
-9	<0.1%
-6	0.3%
-4	0.5%
-3	0.7%
-2	4.2%
-1	39.2%
0	54.3%
1	0.5%

Table 5.4: Sentence position of the extarg relative to the connective in the PCC

positions in the PCC relative to their connective sentence is shown in Table 5.4, where -9 means that the *extarg* appeared 9 sentences before the connective, 0 means that the *extarg* is in the same sentence and 1 means that the *extarg* appeared in the sentence following the connective's sentence.

The extraction of the *extarg* thus consists of two sub-tasks; 1) the prediction of the sentence that contains the *extarg* (**sentence prediction**) and 2), the actual extraction of *extarg* tokens (**token extraction**).

Sentence prediction   For the first sub-task, a simple majority vote baseline, predicting the most popular class for every unique connective (differentiating between upper- and lower-case) already scores relatively high, with an accuracy of 86.59. To improve upon this, we train a classifier that uses the embedding of the connective itself, the part-of-speech embedding of the connective's part-of-speech and categorical values for sentence position and path to the root node (in a constituency tree). The word embeddings were trained on Common Crawl and Wikipedia (Grave et al., 2018) and were chosen because of their availability for German, and because they achieved state-of-the-art performance on several popular NLP tasks at the time, by combining character n-grams and token n-grams. We generated the part-of-speech embeddings ourselves using the TIGER corpus (Brants et al., 2004).

Training this on all positions from Table 5.4 results in an accuracy of 94.52. Since for multi-sentence arguments, we consider a prediction correct if the predicted sentence is in the set of actual sentences, the actual performance will be slightly lower. However, since multi-sentence arguments only make up a small portion of the data set (6%, see Table 5.2) and because we are focusing on final, token-based precision and recall for the argument's tokens, we mention this somewhat inaccurate performance just in passing. We use this position classifier throughout the remainder of the experiments reported upon, and like in the *intarg* setup, by design predict single-sentence arguments only.

Token extraction With this classifier in place for the first sub-task, the second sub-task, i.e., actual *extarg* token extraction, can be dealt with. As a baseline, we extract all tokens in the predicted sentence if this is the preceding or following sentence, and all tokens up to the (first) connective token if the predicted sentence is the same sentence as the connective.

Since the majority of *extarg* instances are in the same sentence, we again use both a constituency and dependency tree approach to improve on this baseline. For next or previous sentence cases, both approaches are equal to the baseline, since there is no anchoring in the tree possible if *extarg* is in another sentence than the connective.

For the dependency tree approach, we apply the following rules: If the connective is sentence-initial, all dependencies of the direct head of the connective are extracted. Since this would be the *intarg*, we take the inverse of this set of tokens to be the *extarg*. If the connective is not sentence-initial, we use a classifier to predict whether the *extarg* will precede or succeed the connective. If the classifier predicts the *extarg* to the left of the connective, we find the first verb preceding the connective (traversing the sentence right to left, starting at the connective) and take all dependents of the head of this verb (including the head itself) to be the *extarg*. If no verb was found, we take all tokens to the start of the sentence to be the argument. If the classifier predicts the argument to the right of the connective, we take the dependents of the head of the first verb to the right of the connective (including the head itself) as the argument (or all remaining tokens if no verb was found). To predict whether the *extarg* precedes or succeeds the connective, we used a simple majority vote per connective (differentiating between upper- and lower-case), and obviously always assume the *extarg* to be to the right of the connective if both are in the same sentence and the connective is sentence-initial. The accuracy of this within-sentence position prediction is 78.59.

An example of the dependency-based approach for both the *intarg* and the *extarg* is shown in Figure 5.1, based on the example in (1). In

67

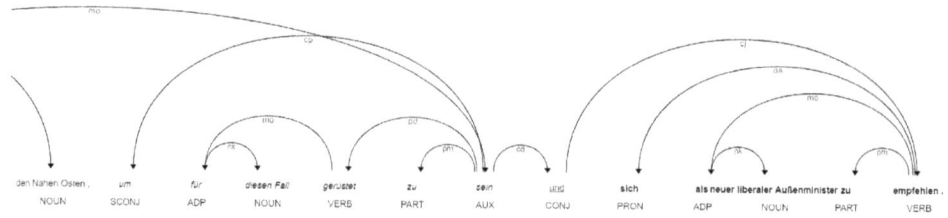

Figure 5.1: Partial dependency tree example

the relevant part of the dependency tree, the connective (underlined) is "und" (*and*), the *intarg* (bold) is extracted by taking all dependents of the head of the connective token "empfehlen" (*recommend*), and the *extarg* (italics) is extracted by finding the first verb to the left of the connective (as per the same sentence classifier's prediction), taking the head of that (*sein*, as we exclude modals in search of the closest verb), and taking all dependents (including the head itself).

For the constituency tree approach, we apply the following rules: If the connective is sentence-initial, we assume that the *intarg* will follow first, as in (32).

(32) <u>Auf Grund</u> **der dramatischen Kassenlage in Brandenburg** *hat sie jetzt eine seit mehr als einem Jahr erarbeitete Kabinettsvorlage überraschend auf Eis gelegt* (maz-00001)
Due to the dramatic cash situation in Brandenburg, she has now surprisingly put on ice a cabinet bill that she had been working on for more than a year

Thus, the first parent node of the connective that is either an S, CS or VP is extracted. We select the right sibling(s) of this node, and take this to be the *extarg*. If the connective is not sentence-initial, we use the same-sentence predictor again. We extract the first parent node of the connective that is either an S, CS or VP and depending on the prediction of the classifier, we take the left sibling(s) or the right sibling(s) of this node to be the *extarg*. For discontinuous connectives[9] we take the tokens in between the first part and the last part, excluding the connective tokens themselves.

The final *extarg* results (combining sentence prediction and token extraction) for the baseline and the dependency and constituency

---

[9]4% of all relations are discontinuous.

	Precision	Recall	F1-score
Baseline	50.41	80.70	61.21
Dependency trees	71.20	**74.60**	**72.80**
Constituency trees	**73.64**	71.73	72.67

Table 5.5: Results for extarg extraction

based approaches are included in Table 5.5, again resulting from 10-fold cross-validation in combination with micro-averaging. In the pipeline setup, using predicted connectives, f1-score drops by 8 points to 64.43, with precision and recall, respectively, at 75.67 and 56.10. To compare, the drop in f1-score for *extarg* extraction reported in Oepen et al. (2016) is 5 points.

5.3.2.1. Results & Evaluation

In the setup using gold standard connectives, the baseline performs worse and both approaches improve by a smaller margin compared to the *intarg* scenario. Moreover, precision and recall for dependencies and constituents show opposite bias on precision and recall, with precision considerably higher than recall for constituents and the opposite scenario, though with a smaller difference, for dependencies. Upon error analysis, we found several cases where conjunctions on S or VP-level were not treated correctly, with again punctuation characters having a conjunction-like role. In the *extarg* case, this seems to be more problematic for the constituents approach (lower recall due to conjuncts being overlooked) than for the dependencies approach.

Looking at f1-score though, in this setup both, approaches perform very much comparably too. This time the dependency-based approach outperforms the constituency-based one, though only by a small margin. Apart from the greater negative impact of punctuation and conjunction for the constituents approach, we generally encountered the same types of errors as in the *intarg* scenario for both approaches. The lower performance can furthermore be explained by error propagation of the relative sentence position classifier; if the wrong sentence has been predicted, every token in that sentence contributes to the false positives and every token in the actual *extarg* to the false negatives. As illustrated in Table 5.4, the vast majority of discourse relations have their *extarg* either in the same sentence, the previous sentence, or the sentence before the previous sentence. In an attempt to increase accuracy of the sentence position classifier, we experimented with simplifying to a three-class classification problem accordingly. This however did not increase the final f1-score. Due to the higher percentage of *extarg* cases being scattered over multiple sentences, our practical limitation of considering only single sentences also has more (negative) impact here.

Because the heuristics around selecting tokens once the position (i.e., sentence) of the *extarg* has been established are very much comparable to the ones for the *intarg* (often times the same rules are applied, followed by tree subtraction to end up at *extarg*), the same sources of errors as in the *intarg* scenario occur here, and re-evaluating by ignoring any punctuation symbols leads to a comparable increase of 0.30 points in f1-score.

One considerable additional source of error for the *extarg* case was instances where the wrong sentence has been predicted by the classifier, amounting to potentially many false negatives (every word of the actual *extarg*) and false positives (every word in the predicted sentence). To gain some insight into *extarg* instances that are not in the current or previous sentence, we looked at all relations where the *extarg* is not adjacent to *intarg* or the connective. Unlike Dines et al. (2005), who study attribution as a source of discontinuous or non-adjacent arguments, we find no such cases (more precisely, we do find one case where attribution occurs, but it is not the main source of non-adjacency). After filtering for punctuation inconsistencies, 15 cases remain where some related information or a fragment serving rhetorical purposes is intervening in between both arguments. A typical example is shown in (33), where again the *extarg* is displayed in italics, the connective underlined and *intarg* in bold face. The intervening material "Warum sollten sie nicht noch einen guten Zweck erfüllen?" (*Why shouldn't it serve a good purpose?*) here has the purpose of a rhetorical question which does not really contribute to the interpretation of the discourse relation.

(33) "*Wohin dann mit den vom Urlaub übrig gebliebenen Münzen, die bald sowieso nichts mehr wert sind?* Warum sollten sie nicht noch einen guten Zweck erfüllen können? <u>So</u> **wurde die Aktion " Euro-Cash for Kids " gestartet,** und sie fand speziell in Luckenwalde und Umgebung eine riesige Resonanz." (maz-8838)

Where to then with the cash remaining from the vacation, which is soon worthless anyway? Why shouldn't it serve a good purpose? Thus, the initiative "Euro-Cash for Kids" was started, and it resonated very well especially in Luckenwalde and surroundings.

5.4. Portability to English

The other components in the pipeline architecture that are described in this dissertation primarily rely on classification models, which in turn rely on annotated data, but whose architecture is not necessarily language-dependent. Because of the rule-based characteristic of this component for argument extraction, giving rise to the question to what extent these rules are language-dependent, we attempt to port this component to English. In particular, to put the numbers discussed Section 5.3.1.1 and 5.3.2.1 into perspective, we apply the same methods for *intarg* and *extarg* extraction to English, using the training section of the 2016 CoNLL shared task.

5.4.1. *Intargs*

We change the set of rules for *intarg* extraction by, in contrast to German, not considering clause-initial and/or clause-final punctuation (if this was not included in the sub-tree already), due to annotation guideline differences between the PCC and the PDTB. Otherwise, the heuristics are directly applied to the English parse trees. The resulting numbers are to be compared to the numbers for *arg2* presented in Table 4 in Oepen et al. (2016): 75.3 and 78.2 for the WSJ test set and the blind set respectively. As noted in Section 5.1, a direct comparison to other approaches is not straightforward either because of a different measure or the effect of error propagation from connective classification. Using the dependency approach (using the spaCy parser with the English model), we get an f1-score of 88.63 (compared to 84.03 for German/PCC) and using the constituency approach (also using the same (NLTK Stanford) parser but with English model), we get 82.58 (compared to 84.35 for German/PCC). One possible explanation for the considerable drop when using constituency trees could be the fact that both prepositions and subordinating conjunctions have the same part-of-speech tag (i.e *IN*). Although the PDTB, in contrast to the PCC, does not include prepositions as connectives, our heuristics were designed with the PCC in mind (which does include prepositions). This could lead certain rules to trigger in unwanted scenarios, although more investigation would be needed to clarify this. The much smaller difference for the dependency-based scenario could be due to more available training data and better models for the English dependency parser (though one would expect the same to be true for the constituency parser). Again, more research would be needed to verify this, but we consider it out of scope as we are focusing on German.

5.4.2. *Extargs*

We train an *extarg* sentence prediction classifier and modify token extraction heuristics for English by changing the German components for English ones (i.e., using the English embeddings from Grave et al. (2018) and the Penn Treebank (Marcus et al., 1993) to generate part-of-speech embeddings for sentence prediction. For token extraction, we use the English dependency and constituency counterparts, as in the *intargs* setup). For the constituency approach, we obtained an f1-score of 59.32 (compared to our 72.67 for German) and for the dependency approach an f1-score of 59.35 (compared to our 72.80 for German). Again consulting Table 4 in Oepen et al. (2016), our scores should be compared to 57.2 and 58.6 for the WSJ test set and the blind set respectively. Given that in the *Arg1* scenario, the position classifier plays a role, and more training data is likely to increase its performance, this significant drop in performance is not what we would have expected. Upon consulting the annotation manuals (Prasad et al., 2007; Stede, 2015), we can find no obvious cause for this discrepancy; both guidelines allow for nominalizations, VP-coordinates or other causes that may lead to annotated spans smaller than typical finite clauses[10] (both syntax-based approaches are biased toward typical finite clauses). Since our focus is on German, we consider a more detailed analysis of this difference an interesting piece of future work, but one that is out of scope for this paper.

---

[10]Note that while the PCC guidelines allow for these constructions, they contain no syntactic directives per se and instruct the annotator to select the minimal token span necessary to interpret the discourse relation without phrasing this in terms of syntactic units.

5.5. Summary

In conclusion, this chapter outlines our approach to the extraction of arguments for explicit relations, once the (position of) connectives are known. We compare a set of heuristics based on dependency trees to a set of heuristics based on constituency trees. In addition, we discuss the effect of error propagation from incorrectly predicted (or missed) connectives, using the classifier from Chapter 4. The idea behind using this set of hand-crafted rules is that this approach is relatively independent of domain. Given the availability of either a constituency or dependency parser, they can be implemented and used; we demonstrate this by porting our approach to English and present results on English data. We re-iterate that the main contribution, as well as tables and figures, are taken from Bourgonje and Stede (2019).

The argument extraction component described in this chapter is the second component in the pipeline for end-to-end shallow discourse parsing. In the next chapter, the next component in the pipeline, that of sense classification, is discussed.

Chapter 6

Sense Classification

Chapters 4 and 5 dealt with the identification of connectives and the extraction of both their arguments. The last sub-task when dealing with explicit relations is the assignment of a particular relation sense to the discourse relation. For this, we obviously need a set of relation senses to choose from. While some fundamental categories or dimensions are non-controversial (like *causal*, *contrastive* and *temporal*) and show up in the inventories of most theories dealing with coherence relations, defining a definitive list, taxonomy or hierarchy of coherence relations is non-trivial, to say the least.

With the introduction of RST (Mann and Thompson, 1988), a set of 23 relations was proposed, though the authors acknowledge that this list may not be complete and includes only "those (relations) which have proven most useful for the analysis of the data we have examined" (Mann and Thompson, 1988, p.7). Inside the RST paradigm, several different relation sets have been used since (Carlson et al., 2002; Hovy and Maier, 1993; Knott, 1996; Rösner and Stede, 1992).[1]

In SDRT (Asher et al., 2003), and more specifically in Reese et al. (2007), a set of 14 relations is used. These relations are grouped first by either coordinating or subordinating relations, then by *veridical* vs. *nonveridical*, where "Veridical relations entail the content of (both of) their arguments, whereas non-verdical relations fail to entail the content of at least one of their arguments" (Reese et al., 2007, p.8).

Sanders et al. (1992) (in the literature referred to as CCR, for a Cognitive approach to Coherence Relations) devise a set of 12 classes

---

[1]A good overview is provided in Section 2 of Das (2014).

of relations, inspired by a psychological/cognitive account and based on four[2] *cognitive primitives* (*basic operation*, *source of coherence*, *order of the segments* and *polarity*, see Sanders et al. (1992) for more details.). More recently, an attempt to reconcile RST, SDRT and PDTB senses, using CCR, has been described in Sanders et al. (2018).

Since we are using the PDTB framework throughout, we also rely on the corresponding sense hierarchy. This started with the relation set used in the first release, in which only implicit relations and alternative lexicalisations were annotated for senses, leaving out explicit relations. The relation set used in the initial release was motivated by the feature-based classification of Knott (1996) and consisted of seven main labels: *Additional-Info*, *Causal*, *Temporal*, *Contrast*, *Condition*, *Consequence* and *Restatement/Summarization*.

The second release annotated senses for explicit relations too, and introduced a sense hierarchy[3]. The idea behind this hierarchy is that the top level *classes* specify the four major semantic classes. The second level of *types* further refines the semantics of the class level, and the third level of *sub-types* specifies the semantic contribution of each argument. For example, the sub-type *reason* is used when the situation specified in the *intarg* is interpreted as the cause of situation specified in the *extarg*, and the sub-type *result* applies if the reverse argument order is the case. The motivation of introducing a hierarchy is two-fold: 1) Ideally, annotators specify the fully detailed (third-level) sense, but the hierarchy (in conjunction with the annotation guidelines) allows them to leave out details, so that they do not have to commit to specifications that cannot be deduced from the text (alone); and 2), it allows inferencing and grouping of detailed relations under their higher level labels. The hierarchy does not claim to capture the entire spectrum of discourse relations and the annotation manual acknowledges that "arguments may also be related to one another in ways that do not have corresponding sense tags" (Prasad et al., 2007, p.26).

The third release of the PDTB introduced minor modifications to the sense hierarchy. Some modifications were aimed at eliminating

---

[2]A fifth dimension, dealing with *temporal order* was added later (Evers-Vermeul et al., 2017).

[3]The list of senses used in the 1.0 version did have one additional level, with sub-classes for *Additional-Info* (*Continuation*, *Elaboration*, *Exemplicitation* and *Similarity*) and for *Contrast* (*Opposition*, *Concession*, and *Denial of Expectation*).

distinctions that proved difficult to annotate (Webber et al. (2019) mentions the sub-type relations under *Contrast*). The result being that the sub-type specifications now only relate to argument order (i.e., *extarg≫intarg* vs. *intarg≫extarg*). In addition, new types and sub-types were added to accommodate intra-sentential relations (see Webber et al. (2019, p.18) for details). The resulting hierarchy is depicted in Figure 6.1.

In line with our annotations, explained in Chapter 2, this PDTB3.0 sense hierarchy is the set of relations we use to train and evaluate our classifier that deals with this final sub-task for explicit relation, which is also referred to in the literature as *sense classification*.

Using the complete hierarchy, this results in an 29-way classification problem.[4] Many approaches to the task however, choose to report performance on the second level of the hierarchy only (rendering it an 17-way classification problem), or even on the first level only, resulting in a 4-way classification problem (see Sections 6.1 and 6.2 for examples).

With the popularisation of embedding-based methods, aiming to capture the semantics of words and phrases, performance for sense classification has improved considerably. The majority of work on this sub-task of sense classification for discourse relations, however, has focused on implicit relations. Due to the presence of the connective, explicit relation classification is considered a much easier task, with many researchers referring to Pitler and Nenkova (2009).

To the best of our knowledge though, there exists no prior work on sense classification for German. The implementation of a baseline, based on state-of-the-art contextualised embeddings methods, and reporting on performance in the PCC is a key contribution of this chapter. In addition, we exploit DiMLex and demonstrate how this improves performance over the baseline. Sections 6.1, 6.2 and 6.3 present related work on the sub-task of sense classification and explain our approach, working on German and the PCC.

6.1. Related Work

An influential approach to explicit relation sense classification is presented by Pitler and Nenkova (2009), reporting an accuracy of 94.15

---

[4]The +/- belief and +/- speech act add-ons are typically implemented as additional features to the sense, not as senses by themselves.

Level-1	Level-2	Level-3
TEMPORAL	SYNCHRONOUS	–
	ASYNCHRONOUS	PRECEDENCE
		SUCCESSION
CONTINGENCY	CAUSE	REASON
		RESULT
		negRESULT
	CAUSE+BELIEF	REASON+BELIEF
		RESULT+BELIEF
	CAUSE+SPEECHACT	REASON+SPEECHACT
		RESULT+SPEECHACT
	CONDITION	ARG1-AS-COND
		ARG2-AS-COND
	CONDITION+SPEECHACT	–
	NEGATIVE-CONDITION	ARG1-AS-NEGCOND
		ARG2-AS-NEGCOND
	NEGATIVE-CONDITION+SPEECHACT	–
	PURPOSE	ARG1-AS-GOAL
		ARG2-AS-GOAL
COMPARISON	CONCESSION	ARG1-AS-DENIER
		ARG2-AS-DENIER
	CONCESSION+SPEECHACT	ARG2-AS-DENIER+SPEECHACT
	CONTRAST	–
	SIMILARITY	–
EXPANSION	CONJUNCTION	–
	DISJUNCTION	–
	EQUIVALENCE	–
	EXCEPTION	ARG1-AS-EXCPT
		ARG2-AS-EXCPT
	INSTANTIATION	ARG1-AS-INSTANCE
		ARG2-AS-INSTANCE
	LEVEL-OF-DETAIL	ARG1-AS-DETAIL
		ARG2-AS-DETAIL
	MANNER	ARG1-AS-MANNER
		ARG2-AS-MANNER
	SUBSTITUTION	ARG1-AS-SUBST
		ARG2-AS-SUBST

Figure 6.1: PDTB3.0 Sense hierarchy (Webber et al., 2019, p.17)

on the PDTB2.0 when classifying for the four top levels. They suggest that "further improvements may not be possible" (Pitler and Nenkova, 2009, p.16), since human inter-annotator agreement on the top level was also 94%. Accordingly, several researchers have interpreted this as sufficient for the time being and in recent years focused on non-explicit relation sense classification instead (see Section 7.1 for an overview).

Sense classification (for both explicit and implicit relations) featured in the end-to-end shallow discourse parsing tasks of CoNLL 2015 and 2016 (Xue et al., 2015, 2016) and moreover featured as a supplementary task in 2016, allowing participants to focus only on this component. The best results for sense classification of explicit relations in 2016 were obtained by Mihaylov and Frank (2016), who achieve an f1-score of 78.20 on the third, most detailed, level of the PDTB sense hierarchy[5], using word2vec (Mikolov et al., 2013) word embeddings and a Logistic Regression classifier. Wang and Lan (2016) achieved second place, with an f1-score of 77.41 for explicit senses. Their explicit sense classification component is based on their system for the 2015 shared task (Wang and Lan, 2015), which in turn exploits a Maximum Entropy classifier in combination with the connective features from Lin et al. (2014) (see Section 4.4.3 for details) and adds five additional features, mostly targeted at the connectives *as* and *when*, which they find to be highly ambiguous in the training set (see Wang and Lan (2015, p.20) for more details). Third place was claimed by Oepen et al. (2016), with an f1-score of 77.17 for explicit senses. Their system uses an ensemble classifier for explicit senses, consisting of a majority class senser, a re-implementation of the Wang and Lan (2015) classifier using an SVM instead of Maximum Entropy classifier, and a Decision Tree classifier.

Beyond the shared task context, Meyer and Popescu-Belis (2012) attempt to improve Machine Translation performance by disambiguating connectives. They ignore the third level of the PDTB sense hierarchy, claiming that the information conveyed there is too fine-grained for their use case of English-French translation. Thus classifying on the second level, they report an f1-score of 75 when classifying a subset of 13 temporal and contrastive connectives, using syntactic features, WordNet relations and candidate translations.

---

[5]The team from IIT-Hyderabad achieved a slightly higher score of 78.42, but they had not submitted a system description paper.

For German, to the best of our knowledge, no prior work on sense classification (explicit or implicit) exists.

6.2. Explicit Senses in the Potsdam Commentary Corpus

This section provides a brief overview of all explicit relations in the PCC. Recall from Chapter 2 that 50.5% of all relations in the PCC are explicit. Table 6.1 illustrates the distribution over the four top levels, and Figure 6.2 shows the more detailed distribution, including the second and third level of the sense hierarchy. Since the PDTB is the nearest neighbour of the data we include this overview for the PDTB as well in Figure 6.3.

Top level sense	Frequency	Relative frequency
Comparison	277	26%
Contingency	329	29%
Expansion	415	37%
Temporal	91	8%
Total	1,112	100%

Table 6.1: Top level sense distribution of explicit relations in the PCC2.2

As Table 6.1 illustrates, apart from *Temporal* being by far the least frequent top level class, the other three have a relatively comparable distribution. When looking at the more detailed types and sub-types in Figure 6.2 though, especially for *Comparison* and *Expansion*, there is one particular sense that stands out (*Comparison.Concession.Arg2-as-denier* and *Expansion.Conjunction*, respectively), and the others in the respective top levels are seldom occurring.

When working on the PDTB, some researchers report results using the fully specified senses (the 2015 and 2016 CoNLL shared task submissions discussed in Section 6.1), some report results ignoring the third level of sub-types (Lin et al., 2014; Rutherford et al., 2017; Shi and Demberg, 2019)[6] and some only use the four top level senses for training and evaluation (Ji and Eisenstein, 2015; Pitler and Nenkova, 2009).

While we are working on German and are using considerably less data, to facilitate comparison, we include all three flavours and report

---

[6]Note that Rutherford et al. (2017); Shi and Demberg (2019) work on implicit relations though.

Figure 6.2: Sense distribution of explicit relations in the PCC2.2

results using only the four top level senses, the second level of the hierarchy and the fully specified third level.

6.3. Classifying Explicit Senses

For the classification of senses for explicit relations, we basically exploit the same setup as the one used in connective classification, as explained in Section 4.4. The baseline relies on contextualised embeddings and we attempt to improve upon this by exploiting infor-

Figure 6.3: Sense distribution of explicit relations in the PDTB3.0

mation from DiMLex and additional syntactic information (from the data itself). Similarly to the connective classification scenario, we attempt to find out to what extent both knowledge- (e.g., DiMLex) and linguistically-informed (e.g., syntax tree-based rules) methods can augment a contextualised embeddings-based approach. Especially since the amount of data used for fine-tuning to particular tasks in Devlin et al. (2019) is still significantly higher than the numbers we have available for training (see Section 4.4.1). The baseline and the setups exploiting DiMLex and syntactic information are described in Sections 6.3.1 to 6.3.3.

6.3.1. Baseline

The baseline setup is identical to the connective identification setup. It uses the base version of a German BERT model[7], which returns a 786-dimensional vector for a given input sequence. We obtain this vector for both arguments of the connective and concatenate this in order of appearance (i.e., either *extarg≫intarg* or *intarg≫extarg*). In addition, we retrieve the vector for the connective itself. The reason for including the embedding for the connective (in isolation) is to differentiate between connectives with identical (or nearly identical) arguments, but different senses, that would otherwise have (near-)identical representations. Consider example (34):

(34) Justice Stevens, 69, is probably the most philosophical of the dissenters about his role, in part because he may be the least liberal of the four, but also because he enjoys the intellectual challenge of arguing with the majority more than the others. (wsj_2347)

In the PDTB, "but" and "also" have an identical *Arg1* ("in part because he may be the least liberal of the four") and a near-identical *Arg2* ("also because he enjoys the intellectual challenge of arguing with the majority more than the others" and "but because he enjoys the intellectual challenge of arguing with the majority more than the others", for "but" and "also", respectively), but different senses; *Comparison.Concession.Arg2-as-denier* for "but" and *Expansion.Conjunction* for "also". Including the embedding of the connective in isolation allows the classifier to better differentiate between the two.

Since the base version of our BERT model returns a 786-dimensional vector, we concatenate the obtained representations for our three input sequences (two arguments plus a connective) into a 2304-dimensional vector. This is then fed as input to a MultiLayer Perceptron classifier, with the annotated sense as label. Results are reported for the

---

[7]https://deepset.ai/german-bert

four top level senses, for the second level of types, and for the fully specified senses, including sub-types.

6.3.2. DiMLex

The DiMLex setup combines the baseline, using BERT, with information coming from DiMLex. Recall from Chapter 2 that for every entry, DiMLex specifies the sense(s) it can express. For some entries, information on particular frequency distribution is available, in the case where it can express multiple senses. Because this is coming from a relatively small amount of annotations, and crucially is not present for all entries, we refrain from using this as an extra probability indicator. This setup thus uses the prediction from the baseline setup and, as a post-processing step, overrules this in case an assigned sense is not compatible with information from DiMLex for the corresponding connective.

Another advantage of this procedure is that we can predict the sense for unambiguous connectives that, due to very low frequency, appear in the test data, but not in the training data. A purely empirically based approach would have to assign some particular out-of-vocabulary or popular vote sense in this case. Using DiMLex, for unambiguous connectives we select the correct sense, and for ambiguous connectives we can randomly select one from the list of possible senses. Since there are 52 singletons in the PCC, the case where the instance is in the test set alone occurs 52 times (4.6% of all explicit relations).

6.3.3. DiMLex & Syntactic Features

In an attempt to further improve performance, we combine both the baseline and the exploitation of DiMLex with a set of manually crafted features. We use the feature set from Bourgonje and Stede (2018a), which in turn is based on the syntactic features from Pitler and Nenkova (2009). Recall from Section 4.2 that this feature set includes surface level and part-of-speech bigrams, the categories of a connective's parent node and that of its left and right siblings, whether or not the right sibling contains a VP, and the path to the root node. The values for these features are based on constituency trees obtained from the German Stanford LexParser (Rafferty and Manning, 2008). Since both feature sets contain information of a different kind, and crucially have different dimensions, we combine predictions from the MultiLayer Perceptron classifier from the baseline and a RandomForest classifier (based on earlier success using a RandomForest classifier for syntactic features (Bourgonje and Stede, 2018a)) for the additional features, and average their predictions. The information from DiMLex is used as a post-processing step, as explained in Section 6.3.2.

6.4. Results & Evaluation

The accuracy scores for all three setups explained in Section 6.3 are included in Table 6.2. All scores are the result of 10-fold cross-validation.

	Top level	Second level	Third level
Baseline	83.01	76.43	74.52
DiMLex	85.05	**81.67**	**80.49**
DiMLex & Syntactic features	**85.63**	80.57	79.29
DiMLex (error propagation)	57.86	54.65	54.11

Table 6.2: Results for sense classification on the PCC

In contrast to connective identification (see Table 4.3), for sense classification, after exploiting information from DiMLex, adding syntactic information generally does not improve performance (except when considering top level senses only). This contrasts with earlier findings by Nayak et al. (2013), who found that a RandomForest classifier performed particularly well in a multi-label setup (for sense classification we have multiple labels, whereas we have a binary set for connective identification). We can find no explanation for this discrepancy. In the pipeline architecture implementation, only the setup combining BERT with DiMLex (the second row in Table 6.2) is implemented, and the fourth row represents scores with error propagation from the connective classification and argument extraction modules. This illustrates the severe impact of error propagation of both connective identification and argument extraction.

Table 6.3 presents the scores for the Wikipedia & News data. For this data, we used the entire PCC for training and the entire Wikipedia & News data for testing, and only implemented the DiMLex setup. For this data, the impact of error propagation is less severe (a ca. 15-point drop for the third level, compared to a ca. 25-point drop for the PCC setup), but of course the starting point is considerably lower already.

	Top level	Second level	Third level
DiMLex	68.47	52.42	47.32
DiMLex (error propagation)	45.43	35.74	32.55

Table 6.3: Results for sense classification on the Wikipedia & News data

6.5. Summary

This chapter outlines our approach to the sense classification of explicit relations, once the connectives and their arguments are extracted. Results when using gold standard connectives and arguments, as well as predicted connectives and arguments (see Chapters 4 and 5), are included. We start with a baseline that exploits contextualised embeddings, based on BERT and demonstrate that this purely empirical approach can be improved by post-processing the output according to information available in DiMLex. We experiment with an ensemble classifier by combining BERT with syntactic features in the tradition of Pitler and Nenkova (2009), but this does not appear to help at the sense classification level.

This chapter presents, to the best of our knowledge, the first results for the sense classification of explicit relations for German. To facilitate comparison of potential future attempts, we include results when using only the top level, the second level, and the fully specified third level of the PDTB3.0 sense hierarchy. In addition to introducing results for German, a key contribution of this chapter is in demonstrating how empirical approaches, relying on the availability of training data, can be augmented with linguistic information encoded in a connective lexicon. Parts of this chapter are taken from work that has been published earlier (Bourgonje and Stede, 2020a).

The component described in this chapter is the third component in the pipeline for end-to-end shallow discourse parsing, following the upstream tasks of connective identification and argument extract. In Chapter 7, the next component in the pipeline, dealing with implicit relations, is discussed.

Chapter 7

Implicit Relations

With the previous chapters focusing on explicit relations, now we turn to look at the last component in the pipeline, dealing with implicit relations. In the same way that our definition of connectives has profound impact on how to go about processing them, so what it means to be an explicit or implicit relation has far-reaching implications. The definition we use is adopted from the PDTB2.0 annotation guidelines, i.e., "relations between abstract objects that are not realized explicitly in the text (by one of a set of the lexically-defined Explicit connectives)" (Prasad et al., 2007, p. 17). From the literature we know that the distinction between explicit and implicit relations is not as black-and-white as it may seem and has been operationalised in the PDTB. In RST for example, there is no such distinction between explicit and implicit relations and work on how these relations are signalled (Das and Taboada, 2018) in the RST-DT (Carlson et al., 2002) has attempted to identify several other types of signals (other than connectives), including lexical chains, punctuation symbols, meronymy, parallel syntactic constructions, and many more. Other work approaches the difference between both relation types from either a psycholinguistic perspective (Mulder, 2008; Sanders and Noordman, 2000) or a computational perspective (Lapata and Lascarides, 2004; Marcu and Echihabi, 2002; Sporleder and Lascarides, 2005). Due to the limited availability of annotated discourse relations in corpora in the first place, with a distinction between relation types further decreasing available training data volumes for these types, treating the two types in a similar way has been explored in Malmi et al. (2018) and Sporleder and Lascarides (2008), where the latter publication provides a good overview and discussion of the advantages and disadvantages of doing so. More specifically, (Sporleder and Lascarides, 2008) found that a classifier trained on explicit relations with their connective (i.e., discourse marker, in their case) removed does not generalise well to implicit relations (or "unmarked" relations, in their case).

Returning to our definition and the PDTB framework, recently the PDTB3.0 has been extended by the introduction of new relation types that acknowledge the nuances between explicit and implicit relations, for example by including the new `AltLexC` relation type, which is used for cases where "within a sentence, a lexico-syntactic construction has been recognized as signalling a discourse relation" (Webber et al., 2019, p. 9). This expands on the PDTB2.0 `AltLex` relations, used for cases where "the relation is alternatively lexicalized by some "non-connective expression"" (Prasad et al., 2007, p.22), by including lexico-syntactic constructions as markers. In addition, it saw the introduction of intra-sentential implicit relations, as already discussed in Chapter 5.

In terms of data, we again rely on the PCC. As per the PCC2.2 release, the implicit relations in the PCC are a combination of PDTB2.0 and PDTB3.0 guidelines. The implicit relation type definition follows PDTB2.0 guidelines, while the sense taxonomy is adopted from PDTB3.0 guidelines. In line with PDTB2.0 guidelines, implicit relations in the PCC have been annotated to link adjacent sentences that are not already linked explicitly. Having arrived at the final component of the pipeline, we already know where to look for implicit relations; and because they have been annotated for adjacent sentences, the task of deciding on the exact argument span is reduced to mere sentence splitting. This effectively means that the processing of implicit relations is reduced to one of classifying their sense, using the PDTB3.0 sense taxonomy.

We use BERT (Devlin et al., 2019) as the basis for the final component in the pipeline, dealing with implicit relations. In order to train and evaluate implicit relations for German, we had to obtain the relevant annotations, which we consider a major contribution of this dissertation. With this already explained in Chapter 2, however, we consider the contribution of this chapter to be less substantial than that of previous chapters. We implement a component for implicit relations to increase usefulness of the end-to-end parser, i.e., so that it does not only cover those relations marked by discourse markers. The procedure is a relatively straightforward one in the sense that we use off-the-shelf tools and do not further experiment with alternative system architectures or parameter settings. Sections 7.1 and 7.2 first briefly provide some details on the distribution of implicit relations in the PCC. Then, in Section 7.3, we explain the setup we use, provide and discuss the results (Section 7.4), and finally provide a short conclusion (Section 7.5).

7.1. Related Work

The previous chapters have demonstrated that a connective is a very informative cue when dealing with explicit relations. It allows using syntactic information related to both the connective and its arguments (e.g., their shape, and position in the tree), and it allows exploitation of a connective lexicon. Using syntactic (Lee et al., 2006; Lin et al., 2009) or word-pair (Pitler et al., 2009) information for implicit relations has already been applied for this task. More recently, (Mikolov et al., 2013) introduced word embeddings, which attempt to capture word-level semantics by modeling their distribution in a large reference corpus. They have since been widely used for the classification of implicit relations and improved state-of-the-art (Mihaylov and Frank, 2016; Qin et al., 2016; Wang and Lan, 2016), to f1-scores of 34.51, 35.38 and 34.18, respectively, for English. Dai and Huang (2018) provides a good overview of work on implicit relation classification after the 2016 ConLL shared task, and report an f1-score of 48.82, though they only use the four top-level senses of the PDTB hierarchy, in contrast to Mihaylov and Frank (2016); Qin et al. (2016); Wang and Lan (2016), who use the full hierarchy.

More recently, contextualised embeddings allow the encoding of not just individual words, but sequences of tokens, which enables more of their semantic structure to be captured (Devlin et al., 2019; Peters et al., 2018; Radford et al., 2019). This has been shown to improve performance for several benchmark NLP tasks, and has also further progressed state-of-the-art for implicit relation classification: Shi and Demberg (2019) use BERT and report an accuracy of 54.82 when using second-level PDTB hierarchy labels.

The difference in setup makes it difficult to compare the different approaches, with using the top-level senses only (Dai and Huang,

2018) resulting in 4-way classification, using the second-level senses (Shi and Demberg, 2019) resulting in 11-way classification, and using the full hierarchy (Mihaylov and Frank, 2016; Qin et al., 2016; Wang and Lan, 2016) resulting in 34[1]-way classification. In our results (Section 7.4), we include results on all three levels of the PDTB sense hierarchy.

For German, to the best of our knowledge, implicit relations have not been worked on before, and in this chapter we present the first results on German, using the PCC.

7.2. Implicit Relations in the Potsdam Commentary Corpus

This section provides a brief overview of the relation types in the PCC, repeating those numbers from Chapter 2 that are relevant for the processing of implicit relations. For more details on the annotation procedure and resulting agreement figures, we refer back to Chapter 2.

The distribution of the different relation types in the PCC is illustrated in Table 7.1.

	PCC2.2	
AltLex	96	4.4%
EntRel	56	2.5%
Explicit	1,112	50.5%
Implicit	905	41.1%
NoRel	35	1.6%
Total	**2,204**	**100%**

Table 7.1: Distribution of relations in the PCC2.2

This inventory of relations is based on the PDTB2.0, and with 905 implicit relations (ca. 41% of all relations), this approximates the distribution in the PDTB2.0, where this figure is ca. 40%.

Table 7.2 displays the distribution of the four top-level senses in the PCC, with the inventory of relation senses being taken from the PDTB3.0[2] (see Chapter 6).

---

[1]The exact number depends on whether the features Belief and SpeechAct are implemented as their own labels, or dealt with as additional features in a

Top level sense	Frequency	Relative frequency
Comparison	99	11%
Contingency	246	27%
Expansion	540	60%
Temporal	20	2%
Total	**905**	**100%**

Table 7.2: *Top level sense distribution of implicit relations in the PCC 2.2*

A more detailed picture is included in Figure 7.1, illustrating the similarly unbalanced distribution across the second and third level of the PDTB3.0 sense hierarchy. Furthermore, on the second level the PCC only contains 11 classes of the in total 17 distinguished classes, i.e., the remaining six classes were never annotated. The third level, which specifies argument order (either *extarg » intarg* or *intarg » extarg*), is equally sparsely represented in the PCC, i.e., 12 of the in total 29 distinguished classes were never annotated. For completeness' sake, we include the same overview again for the PDTB in Figure 7.2.

In addition to displaying the distribution over the data set, Figure 7.1 illustrates the low frequency of some classes, with four classes occurring only once (*Expansion.Manner.Arg1-as-manner*, *Expansion. Manner.Arg2-as-manner*, *Temporal.Asynchronous.Succession* and *Temporal.Synchronous*). This means that they are either in the training set or in the test set, but never in both. Section 7.3 outlines our method to classify this sparsely populated and unbalanced data set.

7.3. Method

To classify the senses of implicit relations in the PCC, we use a German version of BERT[3], pretrained on a combination of Wikipedia, legal and news texts. To fine-tune this pre-trained BERT model, we adopt the system architecture for paraphrase detection, which is offered as one of three pre-defined tasks for fine-tuning (the other two being question answering and logical inferencing based on natural lan-

---

post-processing step.

[2]The top level remains unchanged going from the PDTB2.0 to the PDTB3.0, though.

[3]https://deepset.ai/german-bert

Figure 7.1: Sense distribution of implicit relations in the PCC2.2

guage) on the BERT GitHub repository[4]. As demonstrated by Devlin et al. (2019), in the fine-tuning phase, the model can learn a variety of different tasks due to its self-attention mechanism. We adopt the system architecture of the paraphrase detection task since the input resembles our own (i.e., two sentences in the paraphrase detection

---

[4]https://github.com/google-research/bert

Figure 7.2: Sense distribution of implicit relations in the PDTB3.0

task; two adjacent sentences in our classification task). The adjacent sentence pairs thus form the input of the classifier and instead of using binary labels, we use the sense labels, rendering this an *n*-way classification problem. Though considerably increasing the number of labels may result in different parameter settings to be optimal, we did not experiment with this and only modified the data to fit the required format.

To facilitate comparison to other (future) approaches, we report results on all three levels of the sense hierarchy. Because not all senses are present in the PCC, this means, in our n-way classification problem, an n of 4 for top-level classification, an n of 11 on the second level and an n of 17 on the third level. The results for both setups are provided and discussed in Section 7.4.

7.4. Results & Discussion

Table 7.3 illustrates the performance on all three levels of the PDTB sense hierarchy on the PCC, split up using the annotated implicit relations (Gold standard implicit relations) and the implicit relations as predicted (by the absence of predicted explicit relations) by the pipeline architecture (Predicted implicit relations). Accuracy scores are the result of 10-fold combination, with micro-averaging.

	Top level	Second level	Third level
Gold standard implicit relations	52.09	31.53	29.61
Predicted implicit relations	47.58	26.59	24.87

Table 7.3: Accuracy for sense classification of implicit relations in the PCC 2.2

This performance, with a difference of 17 to 20 points compared to English (Shi and Demberg, 2019), shows that considerably more instances are needed for the classifier to learn how to classify the data properly. For two of the four top-level classes (*Comparison* and *Temporal*), the label was never predicted in any of the test sets. Given their low frequency (96 and 20 instances, respectively), this is perhaps not surprising. Furthermore, the difference between the second level and the third level performance is rather small. Section 7.1 reported larger differences for this coarse vs. fine grained (second level vs. third level) setup. As shown in Figure 7.1 though, all top level senses have one or two highly populated sub-classes, with the others having very low frequency. This reduces the impact of dropping the third level of the sense hierarchy, explaining the small difference in performance.

In an attempt to establish what performance might be expected for a particular number of samples, we applied the same setup[5] to the PDTB and iteratively down-sampled the number of training instances (randomly, i.e., without considering the distribution of relation types or senses). Figure 7.3 illustrates the result, where the single dot represents performance for German and the dotted line represents performance for English. Using all 12,059 (100%) implicit relations in the PDTB2.0, this results in an accuracy of 46.08. The 905 implicit relations in the PCC amount up to ca. 7% of all PDTB implicit relations, and extrapolating the line to this data size amounts to a very comparable score, suggesting that there is no fundamental difference between the German and English data in this respect, and that providing more training samples would be the most straight-forward way to improve performance.

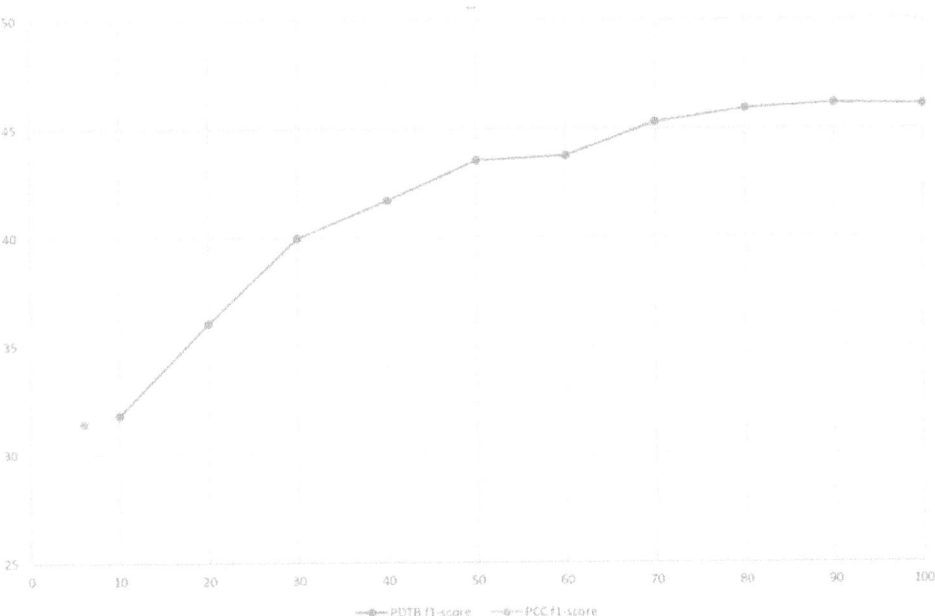

Figure 7.3: Data volume plotted against performance for implicit relation classification

---

[5]But with an English BERT model.

7.5. Summary

This chapter explains our approach to the sense classification of implicit relations in the PCC. We use an off-the-shelf tool (BERT) and do not experiment with parameter settings or alternative system architectures to improve performance. Instead, we conclude that the most promising strategy to improve performance is by creating (i.e., annotating) more training instances, and demonstrate expected performance gain by successively down-sampling English annotations. The main purpose of including this component in the pipeline (and thus adding this chapter) is to increase usability of the end-to-end shallow discourse parser, by not completely ignoring implicit relations, and to provide a basic model for others to experiment with and build on. The comparatively low output quality of this component means that downstream tasks exploiting the parser output should consider ways of dealing with this. One such way would be to assign rather low confidence to the implicit classification output scores. The strategies to combine modern machine learning techniques with linguistic feature-engineering and knowledge representation that are elsewhere used in this dissertation, focus on connectives, and therefore have little use when dealing with implicit relations.

Chapter 8

Connective Lexicons

A connective lexicon as an external resource plays an important role in the shallow discourse parser developed for the purpose of this dissertation. Chapters 4 and 6 have demonstrated that exploiting such a lexicon as an external knowledge base improves performance. Because our parser works on German only, we include this chapter on how to build or improve connective lexicons. In this way, our approach to lexicon generation and development can be replicated for languages for which annotated data is available (see Section 2.1 for an overview), and thus to extend the shallow discourse parser itself for use on languages other than German.

A discussion of different definitions of discourse connectives and early attempts at gathering lists of discourse markers, cue phrases or connectives has already been provided in Section 4.1. This chapter focuses on the strategies for lexicon population (either from scratch, or from a validation point of view, i.e., completing an already existing lexicon) following the DiMLex paradigm, which is to list exhaustively all connectives of a particular language, and for every entry, specify a series of properties relating to surface form, syntax and semantics. Sections 8.1 to 8.2.3 discuss existing lexicons for other languages, different strategies for lexicon population, and the contributions to improving DiMLex and other connective lexicons during the course of this dissertation. These contributions have been previously published in Bourgonje et al. (2017, 2018); Das et al. (2018); Sluyter-Gäthje et al. (2020).

8.1. Related Work

As noted in Section 2.3, DiMLex was the first connective lexicon specifically designed to be both human- and machine-readable. For more details on DiMLex, we refer to Section 2.3, and in this section discuss other lexicons following the DiMLex paradigm. Roze et al. (2012) introduce LEXCONN, a French lexicon of discourse connectives. LEXCONN contains 328 entries and, for every entry, specifies syntactic type (one of the following: co-ordinating conjunction, sub-ordinating conjunction, preposition and adverbial) and semantic type, following the SDRT relation inventory. Roze et al. (2012) started from various corpora of sub-ordinating conjunctions and prepositions, the list of French discourse markers resulting from ANNODIS (Péry-Woodley et al., 2011), and they translated the list of English cue phrases from Knott and Dale (1994) into French. The final lexicon was the result of manual curation of these resources. Mírovský et al. (2016) presents CzeDLex, a Czech lexicon of discourse connectives containing 205 entries. A draft version has been automatically extracted from the Prague Discourse Treebank (Rysová et al., 2016) and this has been manually checked. CzeDLex uses the PDTB sense inventory and for every entry additionally lists its English equivalent. Feltracco et al. (2016) introduce LICo, an Italian lexicon listing 173 entries including orthographic variants for each entry, and using the PDTB sense inventory. Feltracco et al. (2016) started out with lists of connectives (Ferrari, 2010; Sabatini-Coletti, 2005) and combined this with (manual) translations of the entries in DiMLex to arrive at the final lexicon. Mendes and Lejeune (2016) present LDM-PT, a Portuguese lexicon of discourse markers. LDM-PT contains 210 entries; the authors used a parallel corpus (Europarl (Koehn, 2005)) and spotted discourse markers in the English sentences, then checked the Portuguese sentences for potential entries for the lexicon. LDM-PT uses the PDTB sense inventory and opposed to the other lexicons mentioned here, it also includes alternative lexicalisations in the PDTB tradition. Das et al. (2020) introduce a lexicon of Bangla discourse markers (DiMLex-Bangla), containing 123 entries. These have been sourced from traditional Bangla grammars and by translating the items in DiMLex-Eng into Bangla. After generating this initial list, the Bangla RST Discourse Treebank (under construction at the time of writing this dissertation, see Das et al. (2020) for details) was used as well. DiMLex-Bangla uses both PDTB3.0 and RST senses for its entries.

Maschler (2002) describes work on Hebrew discourse markers, but this work did not result in a human- and machine-readable lexicon conveniently listing the properties of its entries. A list of Spanish discourse particles is available online[1], with its corresponding publication (Briz et al., 2008) available in Spanish only[2]. Other work, which has resulted in an Arabic lexicon is described in Keskes et al. (2014), but without particular focus on the lexicon generation process.

Table 8.1 alphabetically lists all lexicons described in this section, and also includes DiMLex-Eng and DisCoDict, which are described in more detail in Sections 8.2.1 and 8.2.2, respectively.

Lexicon Name (Language)	Number of Entries
CzeDLex (Czech)	205
DiMLex (German)	275
DiMLex-Bangla (Bangla)	123
DisCoDict (Dutch)	207
DiMLex-Eng (English)	149
LDM-PT (Portuguese)	210
LEXCONN (French)	328
LICo (Italian)	173

Table 8.1: Connective lexicons for various languages

The above-mentioned lexicons, with the exception of the Spanish list of discourse particles, are all available in a central platform hosted online[3] and described in Stede et al. (2019). Note that the versions hosted on this platform may deviate from their original versions. Most notably, a syntactic and semantic mapping was carried out to translate the lexicon's individual syntactic categories to the five main types of co-ordinating and sub-ordinating conjunctions, prepositions, adverbials and an 'other' category. The semantic mapping maps the lexicon sense inventory to PDTB3.0 senses[4].

The platform allows multi-lingual search of connectives by string, syntactic category or sense and a screenshot of the GUI is included

---

[1]http://www.dpde.es

[2]Unfortunately, the author of this dissertation does not speak or read Spanish.

[3]http://connective-lex.info/

[4]Only LEXCONN originally does not use PDTB senses, but others may use PDTB2.0 senses, in which case they were mapped to PDTB3.0 senses.

in Figure 8.1.

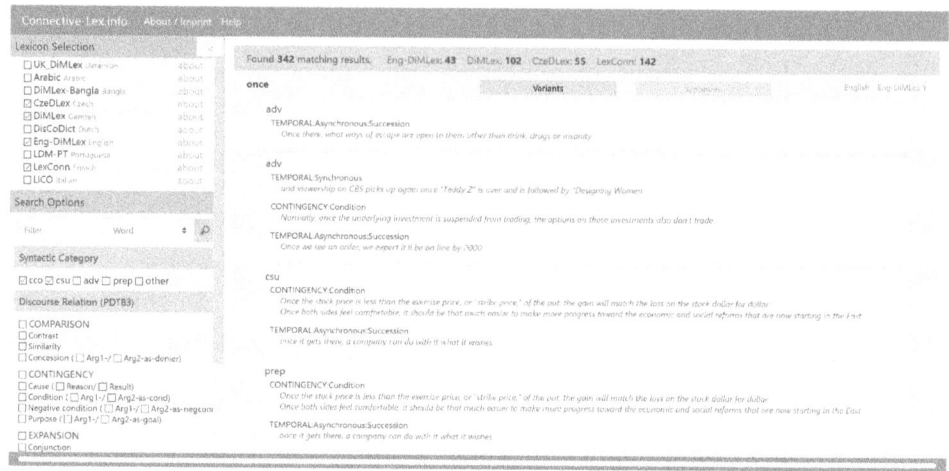

Figure 8.1: Screenshot of the Connective-lex.info GUI

8.2. Strategies for Lexicon Population

Section 8.1 already mentioned several different ways of creating a lexicon. The same methods that can be used to create a lexicon can also be used to verify or complete an already existing one, and in the following subsections, both creation from scratch (Sections 8.2.1 and 8.2.2) and validation (Section 8.2.3) are discussed.

For both the population and validation of connective lexicons, four main strategies can be distinguished:

- Using traditional grammars or lexicons to compile a list of candidates.

- Translating an existing connective lexicon from another language.

- Using an annotated corpus to extract a list of candidates. Ideally, the annotated corpus is already in the lexicon target language. Alternatively, this approach can be used in conjunction with annotation projection.

- Compiling a list of candidate entries from native speaker intuition.

For the creation of a lexicon from scratch, most authors use a combination of these. Using a native speaker's intuition can be particularly useful for validation, or for finding orthographic variations that are very rare or archaic and unlikely to show up in a corpus. By itself however, compiling a list from native speaker intuition is not likely to result in an exhaustive list of connectives. Of the six lexicons mentioned in Section 8.1, four (LEXCONN, LICo, DiMLex-Bangla and DiMLex) use traditional grammars or other resources to populate the list of candidate entries. Three lexicons collected candidates by translating another connective lexicon (DiMLex-Eng in the case of DiMLex-Bangla, DiMLex in the case of LICo, and the list of cue phrases from Knott (1996) in the case of LEXCONN). These two methods are mostly used in combination[5].

Two lexicons were extracted from annotated corpora only. CzeDLex is extracted from the Prague Discourse Treebank (Rysová et al., 2016) and, because of the multi-layer characteristic of this corpus, additional information relating to syntax (part-of-speech tags) or semantics (relation sense) could be extracted automatically along with the candidate entries. This is probably the most efficient and least labour-intensive way of populating a lexicon (and is also the main strategy used for DiMLex-Eng, which exploits the PDTB and the RST Signaling Corpus (Das, 2014), see Section 8.2.1 for more details), but of course presupposes the existence of such an annotated corpus. LDM-PT is extracted from EuroParl (Koehn, 2005) in combination with the explicit connectives from the PDTB (100 unique tokens), by spotting the English connectives in the English sentences and manually going over the aligned Portuguese sentences to compile a list of candidates. This corpus-driven approach can be improved by exploiting word alignments (as opposed to just sentence alignments) to decrease the amount of manual labour. Exploiting word alignments has been explored by Versley (2010) and Laali and Kosseim (2014), and is also applied to LICo (see Section 8.2.3). Furthermore, by pattern-matching for English connectives, the non-connective readings are considered; filtering out non-connective instances would be another way to improve the procedure. Alternatively, an annotated corpus can be exploited by (machine-)translating the corpus itself, and using annotation projection to identify candidates in the target

---

[5]Figure 1 in Feltracco et al. (2016, p.3) conveniently illustrates the contribution of each of the individual methods/resources for LICo.

language. This has been explored in Sluyter-Gäthje et al. (2020), where the creation of a German version of the PDTB was the main goal, but the validation of DiMLex a by-product. The idea of using (machine) translation to disambiguate discourse connectives with regard to their sense, dubbed the "translation-spotting technique", has been explored in Cartoni et al. (2013); Meyer et al. (2012). This can be helpful to collect semantic (i.e., sense) information for lexicon candidates, but additional word alignment is required to find these candidates in the first place.

8.2.1. DiMLex-Eng

As part of the contribution of this dissertation, we collaborated in the creation of an English connective lexicon. This work has been previously published in Das et al. (2018). In this project, we started by extracting all 100 explicit connective types from the PDTB, along with their syntactic and semantic information, which could be extracted from the PDTB as well. To further expand the list of candidate entries, we extracted all connectives and other (explicit) discourse markers from the RST Signaling Corpus (RST-SC) (Das, 2014). Though this is annotated over the same WSJ documents as the PDTB, Das (2014) annotated all RST relations in the RST-DT (Carlson et al., 2002) for a wide range of signals, including connectives, lexical chains, particular syntactic constructions, and many more. This resulted in 201 candidates, which of course overlapped with the 100 types extracted from the PDTB. Finally, we used the relational indicator list of Biran and Rambow (2011), who automatically extracted a list of 230 n-grams that frequently co-occur with relations in the RST-DT.

The resulting list of candidate entries was first filtered manually. Whereas all explicit connectives extracted from the PDTB ended up in the final lexicon, many entries from the RST-SC were discarded on the basis of our connective definition (the same as the one used for DiMLex, see Section 2.3). These included symbols of punctuation, infinitival clause constructions and several others. Similarly, many of the entries from the relational indicator list from Biran and Rambow (2011) were excluded by the same definition. This list contained items belonging to different lexical categories, such as nouns (*statement, result*), verbs (*concluded, to ensure*) or other elements which simply comprise random strings of words and do not neatly represent any syntactic constituents (e.g., *and we certainly do, and just as we*).

Merging these lists, we observed that of the 100 PDTB connectives included in the initial version of DiMLex-Eng, 71 connectives are also found in the RST-SC. From the RST-SC, we added 46 connectives which were not present in the list extracted from the PDTB. From the relational indicator list, seven items overlapped with the 46 items already selected from the filtered RST-SC list, and 12 items were already in the list extracted from the PDTB. Of the 230 items in this list, we ended up including only five items. The reason for this relatively low number of additional entries is that relations are often realised without any explicit connective, thus lowering their co-occurrence numbers, to the advantage of other n-grams which may or may not be indicative of the relation, but certainly are not connectives under any definition.

The syntactic information (part-of-speech tags) could for almost all entries automatically be extracted from their original source (both the PDTB and the RST-DT contain this information). The remaining entries were manually specified. For the sense information, we used the PDTB3.0 sense inventory. For the connectives coming from the PDTB2.0, their senses from the corpus thus had to be translated to PDTB3.0 senses. For entries coming from the RST-SC, their RST senses were mapped to PDTB3.0 senses. Both translations were done manually. For the remaining entries coming from the list of relational indicators, senses were added from native speaker intuition.

The resulting connective lexicon of 149 entries is available online[6] and is also hosted on the Connective-lex.info platform.

8.2.2. DisCoDict

Contributing to the creation of a Dutch connective lexicon was equally part of the contribution of this dissertation and this work has been previously published in Bourgonje et al. (2018). In this project, we used DiMLex in combination with two parallel corpora to extract a list of candidate entries. We used the German-Dutch section of EuroParl (Koehn, 2005) and News-Commentary11 (Tiedemann, 2012) to create word alignments for these sentence-aligned corpora, using MGIZA++ (Gao and Vogel, 2008). Using DiMLex entries as a seed list, we checked the words or phrases that were aligned to these entries and applied a frequency (of alignment) threshold. This list was

---

[6]https://github.com/discourse-lab/en_dimlex

then manually filtered for irrelevant entries. Because German and Dutch are relatively similar from both a grammatical and lexical perspective, the quality of the word alignments was relatively good. Frequently, the reason for removing an entry from the list of candidates was because it was a superset of the seed entry, often in combination with punctuation symbols (e.g., *gemäß* (accordingly) aligned to , *overeenkomstig*, where the word was correct, but the comma not part of the connective). Or the entry was a subset of the seed entry (e.g., *umso mehr* (even more) aligned to *te meer*, whereas the proper connective would be *des te meer*).

After manual filtering, the list of candidates was checked against and further supplied with existing resources for Dutch, particularly Hoek (2018); Pander Maat (2002); Van Wijk and Kempen (1980). The original list after filtering contained 157 entries. After removing duplicate entries and a few non-connective words (mostly stance markers), the three additional lists yielded a set of 137 candidates. 87 of these were also included in the list of 157 original candidates, which means that 55% of the final DisCoDict entries also occurred in the original list, while 64% of the list items also occurred in the first draft version of the DisCoDict lexicon. A comparison of the largely automatically generated list of candidate entries that was the starting point of DisCoDict with the list generated on the basis of other Dutch connective inventories, illustrates both the strengths and the weaknesses of the parallel corpus lookup approach. The parallel corpus method did not yield an exhaustive Dutch lexicon, missing many connectives, including some fairly frequent, prototypical connectives such as *doordat* (because (of that)), *toen* (then), or *ook al* (though). On the other hand, the approach identified more connectives than it missed, and additionally identified many connectives that were not included in existing inventories of Dutch connectives, which mostly focused on single-word expressions. Another benefit is that for the connectives it does identify, the approach also generates syntactic and sense label information that otherwise has to be supplemented by hand.

The additional information with regard to syntax and semantics was supplied manually by three human annotators (all native speakers of Dutch and with extensive experience with coherence relations). The part-of-speech tag was decided upon by a human annotator, supported by the syntactic label of the closest German counterpart of the connective (in DiMLex) and the part-of-speech label attached to it by the Alpino parser (Van Noord, 2006) when parsing the connective's example sentence (extracted along with the candidate, from Koehn (2005) or Tiedemann (2012)). The PDTB3.0 sense was decided upon by a human annotator, supported by the sense label of the closest German counterpart in DiMLex.

The resulting connective lexicon is available online[7] and is also hosted on the Connective-lex.info platform.

8.2.3. LICo

Our contributions to working toward a bilingual German-Italian lexicon of connectives are previously published in Bourgonje et al. (2017). The main goal was to establish the set of Italian connectives that correspond to each of the German connectives, and vice versa. In addition though, this work resulted in the validation of both LICo and DiMLex. We focused on the subset of contrastive connectives only and again exploited EuroParl (Koehn, 2005) to extract word alignments using MGIZA++ (Gao and Vogel, 2008). Of all 31 contrastive connectives from DiMLex, 30 were present in the corpus and we extracted the most frequent alignments. The same was done for the 12 contrastive connectives in LICo. This resulted in alignments illustrated in Figures 2 and 3 of Bourgonje et al. (2017), repeated here in Figures 8.2 and 8.3, respectively.

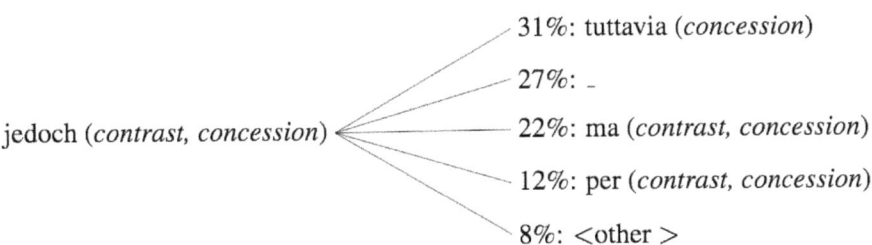

Figure 8.2: Most frequent alignments of jedoch

This bilingual lookup resulted three additional candidates for LICo and two for DiMlex, as well as several orthographic variants for al-

[7]https://github.com/discourse-lab/DisCoDict

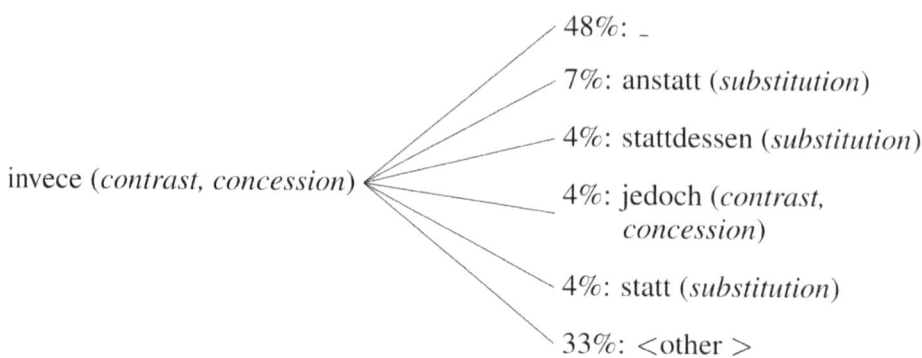

Figure 8.3: Most frequent alignments of invece

ready existing entries. These suggestions were implemented in DiM-Lex, but because we merely used LICo and did not participate in creating (or maintaining) it, the suggestions were communicated to the authors of that resource (Feltracco et al., 2016).

8.3. Extending Lexicon Scope

The size of the connective lexicons discussed in this chapter ranges from 149 (DiMLex-Eng) to 328 (LEXCONN) entries and in most cases the lexicon entries resemble what Danlos et al. (2018) refer to as primary connectives. As discussed in Section 8.2, different strategies have different strengths and weaknesses, and the fact that some lexicons have considerably fewer entries than others could be due to different population strategies. Another factor that plays an important role is validation through usage. Development on DiMLex started with Stede and Umbach (1998) and it has been actively used over the course of more than two decades, resulting in several entries being added since its first release. Whether particular languages really do display more sense ambiguity (resulting in fewer connective types) or use alternative means of signalling discourse relations more extensively than others will have to be verified by further research. The Connective-lex.info platform serves to enable research into exactly this direction, by enabling multi-lingual search and comparison of entries.

The experiments reported upon in this dissertation have demonstrated that using a connective lexicon can considerably improve performance for connective and sense classification, thus improving performance for the umbrella task of shallow discourse parsing. Beyond the prototypical connective lexicon entries however, there is a wide array of alternatives to signal discourse relations (both inside and outside of the PDTB framework), ranging from the secondary connectives of Danlos et al. (2018), which overlap with `AltLex` relations from the PDTB, to a wider interpretation of signals (Das and Taboada, 2018). For the connective identification task, including these lexical, but also syntactical[8] and potentially graphical (Dale, 1991) cues in an extended version of the lexicon could further improve performance. Especially the more data-driven approaches described earlier in this chapter, thanks to their generally higher recall though lower precision, can be helpful in finding such alternative signals, for example by exploiting collocation information (Biran and Rambow, 2011).

For German, due to the absence of `AltLex` relations in the PCC, which would probably be the closest approximation of alternative signaling in the PDTB framework, we cannot empirically verify this. But we consider the inclusion of a broader range of signals in machine-readable connective lexicons as a promising avenue for future work, to further improve parsing performance.

Technically, this can be realised through the use of regular expression entries, where instead of a (long) list of flat string entries, a single entry like `(f|F)or \w+{1,3} reasons?` can be used to capture many different variations (*For this reason, for all these reasons, for this particular reason*). Such regular expression entries would obviously have to be carefully crafted and they may over-match possibilities. The above regular expression will for example also match the last three words in (35).

(35) Besides, Eggers says, grain elevators are worth preserving for aesthetic reasons. (wsj_0102)

However, recall that there are many words in the connective lexicons listed above that are functionally ambiguous, and perhaps indicating both a sentential and discourse reading by default for regular expression entries would prevent false positives on surface forms captured by the regular expression that the author had not considered when writing it.

---

[8]Consider the introduction of the `AltLexC` category in the PDTB3.0 (Webber et al., 2019, p.9).

Apart from regular expressions, another technical extension could be the support of part-of-speech tags, lemma information and/or syntactic phrases, to capture instances like example (36).

(36) Mr. Wertheimer said the Senate Ethics Committee should hire a special outside counsel to conduct an investigation, as was done in the case of former House Speaker James Wright. (wsj_2446)

This of course aligns with the definition of `AltLexC` relations in the PDTB3.0, defined as "a lexico-syntactic construction (...) signalling a discourse relation" (Webber et al., 2019, p.9). For example (35), this has been defined as *<be> <VP/AdjP>*, i.e., any surface form of the verb *to be*, followed by either a verb phrase or an adjectival phrase. This is relatively straightforward to include in a connective lexicon if part-of-speech tags, lemmatisation, and/or higher level syntax information is supported, where for example a universal set of tags can be exploited[9].

8.4. Summary

In conclusion, this chapter discusses connective lexicons for various languages and how they were constructed. We contributed to some of these in the form of creating them from scratch, or by maintaining or updating them. A connective lexicon as an external knowledge base plays an important role in the shallow discourse parser developed for the purpose of this dissertation. In this chapter, we provide perspectives on how to generate or improve such a resource, hoping that this information is useful for others, who either want to replicate the parser architecture, or create such a lexicon for other purposes. This chapter deviates from the schema of Chapters 4 to 7 in that no numerical results are presented. Instead, contributions are highlighted in the corresponding publications (Bourgonje et al., 2017, 2018; Das et al., 2018) or exist in unpublished form (through code commits to the relevant repositories[10] hosting the lexicons).

---

[9]https://universaldependencies.org/u/pos/
[10]https://github.com/discourse-lab/dimlex
https://github.com/discourse-lab/DisCoDict
https://github.com/discourse-lab/DiMLex-Bangla
https://github.com/discourse-lab/en_dimlex

Chapter 9

Conclusion

This final chapter first provides an overview of the theoretical and practical contributions of this dissertation (Sections 9.1 and 9.2) by summarising the contents of the previous chapters. Subsequently, the key findings and most important take-home messages are discussed in Section 9.3. Then, in Section 9.4, an outlook is included on future work and how performance for shallow discourse parsing on German can be improved.

9.1. Theoretical Contributions

Before theoretical contributions to individual sub-tasks can be determined and discussed, the data to test and evaaluate the proposed methods on these sub-tasks has to be present. While this data pre-existed in the form of the 2.0 release of the Potsdam Commentary Corpus, over the course of the last three years, several modifications have been made to the Potsdam Commentary Corpus in the context of working on this dissertation. While the modifications resulting in the PCC2.1 release (see Section 2.2.1) relate to additional annotation layers and making the entire corpus (including new features) available in external tools (Bourgonje and Stede, 2018b), other modifications more directly relate to the final goals of this dissertation, by extending the connectives and arguments layer from the 2.0 version with senses and additional relation types, culminating in the 2.2 release (Bourgonje and Stede, 2020b) (see also Section 2.2.2). In addition to the PCC news commentary data, data has been sourced from Wikipedia and from news articles, and annotated for connectives and their senses. Chapter 2 presents inter-annotator agreement scores on this data and Chapters 4 and 6 present performance on this data.

Following the pipeline processing order, Chapter 4 improves over earlier work on German connective identification. This earlier work focuses on a subset of nine German connectives, though, and we thus present the first across-the-board performance numbers for German connective identification. Our own earlier work includes Bourgonje and Stede (2018a, 2020a), and later modifications of this are included in Chapter 4, leading to a final f1-score for connective identification on the PCC of 87.57. The key contribution of this chapter is the combination of modern contextualised embeddings methods (BERT) with linguistic knowledge encoded into a German connective lexicon (DiMLex), and also the syntactically inspired features of our own earlier work.

Argument extraction for both internal and external arguments is discussed in Chapter 5 and we present the first German performance numbers on discourse relation argument extraction, combining classifiers for external argument position with syntax-based heuristics, experimenting with both constituency and dependency trees. Scores for internal and external argument extraction on the PCC using the different tree types are comparable (with a difference in f1-score of 32 for internal arguments and 13 for external arguments). For internal arguments, the constituency-based approach performs best, with an f1-score of 84.35, while for external arguments, the dependency-based approach performs best, with an f1-score of 72.80. For practical reasons, we implement the constituency-based approach in the end-to-end parser; as the connective identification module uses information from the constituency tree and the input has to be parsed, this information can be re-used for argument extraction. Chapter 5 is based on previously published work (Bourgonje and Stede, 2019).

Sense classification for explicit relations is discussed in Chapter 6. Due to this data not being present for German before, here we present the first results for explicit sense classification for German. The setup is very similar to the one used for connective identification, and the most striking difference is the considerably larger number of labels, corresponding to the items in the PDTB sense hierarchy. We report a final f1-score of 80.49 for the best performing setup, combining BERT representations with linguistic knowledge from DiMLex.

With an overall focus on explicit connectives in this dissertation, we consider the theoretical contribution of Chapter 7 on implicit sense classification to be relatively marginal. We adopt an off-the-shelf architecture for paraphrase detection and, when applying this to the PCC, we report an f1-score of 29.61. Due to this data not being present for German before, these are the first results for implicit sense classification for German. We apply our setup to the English data of the PDTB and iteratively down-sample training data volume and demonstrate that performance for German is comparable to English, when using the same amount of training data.

9.2. Practical Contributions

The practical contribution of this dissertation is aptly summarised by the title. While the theoretical contributions listed above can be, and in fact are, for the purpose of the individual chapters, interpreted as connected, yet modular and relatively independent sub-tasks (exemplified by the fact that gold standard performance can be calculated for every single one of them, using gold standard annotations from upstream sub-tasks), the major practical contribution of this dissertation is the combination of the different modules into a system that works in an end-to-end way. With this, we present the first German end-to-end shallow discourse parser, which is open-source and available to the general public. Its architecture is discussed and explained in Chapter 3, with further usage documentation available in Appendix C.

The focus on connectives in this dissertation is not restricted to the German language and DiMLex. Through the work on the PCC and also DiMLex (both published (Bourgonje et al., 2017; Sluyter-Gäthje et al., 2020) and unpublished), DiMLex has been modified and improved in various steps. But connective lexicons for other languages have also been developed (Bourgonje et al., 2018; Das et al., 2018) and behind the scenes, a multi-lingual platform for connective lexicons[1] has been maintained and expanded, resulting in, at the time of writing this dissertation, connective lexicons for ten different languages. Chapter 8 discusses many of these and provides pointers to strategies for the initial population of new connective lexicons or further refinement of existing connective lexicons.

---

[1]http://connective-lex.info/

9.3. Lessons Learnt

In recent years, deep learning has had a profound impact on various aspects of NLP, improving the state-of-the-art in many different tasks, ranging from machine translation to question answering, text summarisation and natural language generation. Also in shallow discourse parsing itself, the main area of this dissertation, neural network architectures have been proven to be successful, particularly for the sense classification task (see Chapters 6 and 7). This success in the shallow discourse parsing sub-tasks however, thus far remained restricted to English and the PDTB. More generally, deep learning methods have been proven to be successful as long as there is sufficient data to train them on. While recent developments, by pre-training in a self-supervised way and task-specific fine-tuning on annotated data (i.e., in a supervised way), have addressed exactly this problem, the amounts of data needed for successful fine-tuning still exceed the amounts of available annotations for many specific tasks and languages, sometimes by several orders of magnitude.

This stands in contrast to strategies that rely on a human annotator to insert knowledge into the system. This approach, often referred to as a rule-based approach, has lost popularity in the last one or two decades. In this dissertation, we have shown that shallow discourse parsing for German is a complex task with comparatively very little training data available, and that, in such a scenario, linguistic information and knowledge can be beneficial. Either to augment modern machine learning methods and form a hybrid system (Chapters 4 and 6), or as a basis for a set of heuristics, forming a largely rule-based system (Chapter 5).

Whether such strategies are bound to be rendered obsolete by further improvements in deep learning architectures, or whether the pendulum is about to swing back (Church, 2011), remains something for us all to find out in the upcoming years.

Furthermore, throughout this dissertation, we have been in pursuit of the gold standard as dictated by and annotated following the PDTB framework (though for our German data, not for the original, English PDTB data). Chapter 2 already discussed the inter-annotator agreement scores, which are known to be comparatively low for coherence relation annotation tasks. Not only do annotators following the same theory and annotation guidelines often disagree with regard to the correct annotation, different researchers use different theories to describe and analyse coherence relations in the first place. With the PDTB being the most data-driven and corpus-supported of the four main theories briefly described in Section 1.1, corpora following the other frameworks also exist (see Table 4.1). This puts the pursuit of the PDTB gold standard even more into perspective. While we believe the practical and empirically driven approach toward discourse parsing followed in this dissertation is a fruitful pursuit, it is, obviously, not the only feasible strategy, and attempts to bring together the different strands of discourse processing research (either from a theoretical perspective (Sanders et al., 2018) or from a practical perspective (Bourgonje and Zolotarenko, 2019; Zeldes et al., 2019)) are definitely worth pursuing in parallel.

9.4. Outlook

Chapters 4 and 6 have demonstrated the impact of domain transfer, by training on the Potsdam Commentary Corpus and testing on the Wikipedia & News data. Unfortunately, German corpora annotated for discourse relations are very sparse, and to the best of our knowledge, the only other corpus with gold standard annotations that resemble the ones needed to train and test our parser (or its individual modules), is described by Versley and Gastel (2013). An exciting piece of future work would be to evaluate our parser on this data. In parallel, in Sluyter-Gäthje et al. (2020), the PDTB has been translated into German and preliminary experiments with parser evaluation have been performed (Section 6). Following up on suggestions in the final section of Sluyter-Gäthje et al. (2020), effort needs to be put into providing a higher quality translated German-PDTB, which can then possibly be used for training as well (not just evaluation), in order to improve overall performance of the end-to-end German shallow discourse parser.

Another promising direction in order to improve performance seems to be the extension of the connective lexicon that is central to the parsing strategy. As discussed in Section 8.4, DiMLex currently contains what is characterised by Danlos et al. (2018) as *primary connectives*. Given the demonstrated performance gain when using DiMLex for both connective identification and explicit sense classification, further expanding DiMLex along the lines proposed in Section 8.4 could be a fruitful way to further improve general parser performance. Since this would probably first and foremost relate to what in the PDTB have been annotated as `AltLex` and `AltLexC` cases, and these are very rare[2] in the PCC (see Table 2.1), additional annotated data would have to become available first.

---

[2]In fact, so rare that on this ground they have been ignored altogether by our parser.

Appendix A

Potsdam Commentary Corpus Examples

A.1. Tokenized format (tokenized/maz-00001.tok)

Auf Eis gelegt
Dagmar Ziegler sitzt in der Schuldenfalle . Auf Grund der dramatischen Kassenlage in Brandenburg hat sie jetzt eine seit mehr als einem Jahr erarbeitete Kabinettsvorlage überraschend auf Eis gelegt und vorgeschlagen , erst 2003 darüber zu entscheiden . Überraschend , weil das Finanz- und das Bildungsressort das Lehrerpersonalkonzept gemeinsam entwickelt hatten . Der Rückzieher der Finanzministerin ist aber verständlich . Es dürfte derzeit schwer zu vermitteln sein , weshalb ein Ressort pauschal von künftigen Einsparungen ausgenommen werden soll auf Kosten der anderen . Reiches Ministerkollegen werden mit Argusaugen darüber wachen , dass das Konzept wasserdicht ist . Tatsächlich gibt es noch etliche offene Fragen . So ist etwa unklar , wer Abfindungen erhalten soll , oder was passiert , wenn zu wenig Lehrer die Angebote des vorzeitigen Ausstiegs nutzen . Dennoch gibt es zu Reiches Personalpapier eigentlich keine Alternative . Das Land hat künftig zu wenig Arbeit für zu viele Pädagogen . Und die Zeit drängt . Der große Einbruch der Schülerzahlen an den weiterführenden Schulen beginnt bereits im Herbst 2003 . Die Regierung muss sich entscheiden , und zwar schnell . Entweder sparen um jeden Preis oder Priorität für die Bildung .

A.2. Visual Representation of Discourse Relations (based on maz-00001.tok)

Auf Eis gelegt

<rel_12:extarg>Dagmar Ziegler sitzt in der Schuldenfalle .</rel_12:extarg>

<rel_12:intarg><rel_13:extarg>

<rel_1:conn>Auf Grund</rel_1:conn> <rel_1:intarg>der dramatischen Kassenlage in Brandenburg

</rel_1:intarg> <rel_1:extarg><rel_2:extarg>hat sie jetzt eine seit mehr als einem Jahr erarbeitete Kabinettsvorlage überraschend auf Eis gelegt

</rel_1:extarg></rel_2:extarg> <rel_2:conn>und

</rel_2:conn> <rel_2:intarg>vorgeschlagen , erst 2003 darüber zu entscheiden .</rel_2:intarg>

</rel_12:intarg></rel_13:extarg> <rel_4:extarg><rel_5:extarg><rel_13:intarg> Überraschend ,</rel_4:extarg>

<rel_4:conn>weil</rel_4:conn> <rel_4:intarg>das Finanz- und das Bildungsressort das Lehrerpersonalkonzept gemeinsam entwickelt hatten .

</rel_4:intarg></rel_5:extarg></rel_13:intarg> <rel_5:intarg> <rel_14:extarg>Der Rückzieher der Finanzministerin ist <rel_5:conn>aber </rel_5:conn> verständlich .</rel_5:intarg></rel_14:extarg> <rel_14:intarg> <rel_15:extarg>Es dürfte derzeit schwer zu vermitteln sein , weshalb ein Ressort pauschal von künftigen Einsparungen ausgenommen werden soll auf Kosten der anderen .</rel_14:intarg></rel_15:extarg> <rel_15:intarg> <rel_16:extarg>Reiches Ministerkollegen werden mit Argusaugen darüber wachen , dass das Konzept wasserdicht ist .</rel_15:intarg></rel_16:extarg> <rel_16:intarg><rel_17:extarg>Tatsächlich gibt es noch etliche offene Fragen .</rel_16:intarg></rel_17:extarg> <rel_9:extarg><rel_17:intarg>So ist etwa unklar , <rel_7:extarg> wer Abfindungen erhalten soll ,</rel_7:extarg> <rel_7:conn>oder</rel_7:conn> <rel_7:intarg> <rel_8:extarg>was passiert ,</rel_8:extarg> <rel_8:conn>wenn</rel_8:conn> <rel_8:intarg>zu wenig Lehrer die Angebote des vorzeitigen Ausstiegs nutzen .</rel_7:intarg></rel_8:intarg></rel_9:extarg>

</rel_17:intarg> <rel_18:extarg><rel_9:conn>Dennoch</rel_9:conn> <rel_9:intarg> gibt es zu Reiches Personalpapier eigentlich keine Alternative .

</rel_9:intarg></rel_18:extarg> <rel_10:extarg><rel_18:intarg> Das Land hat künftig zu wenig Arbeit für zu viele Pädagogen .

</rel_10:extarg></rel_18:intarg> <rel_19:extarg><rel_10:conn>Und</rel_10:conn> <rel_10:intarg>die Zeit drängt .</rel_10:intarg>

</rel_19:extarg> <rel_19:intarg>
<rel_20:extarg>Der große Einbruch der Schülerzahlen an den weiterführenden Schulen beginnt bereits im Herbst 2003 .</rel_19:intarg>

</rel_20:extarg> <rel_20:intarg>
<rel_21:extarg>Die Regierung muss sich entscheiden , und zwar schnell

.</rel_20:intarg>

</rel_21:extarg> <rel_21:intarg><rel_11:conn>Entweder</rel_11:conn>

<rel_11:extarg>sparen um jeden

Preis</rel_11:extarg> <rel_11:conn>oder</rel_11:conn> <rel_11:intarg>Priorität
für die Bildung .

</rel_11:intarg> </rel_21:intarg>

A.3. PDTB format (connectives/maz-00001.xml)

```
<?xml version='1.0' encoding='UTF
   -8'?>
<?relations relSet="pdtb3" lexURL
   ="jar:file:/home/lisa/Arbeit/
   Conano-Distrib/conano.jar!/de
   /uni_potsdam/ling/coli/
   resources/ConnectorLexicon.xml
   "?>
<discourse>
  <tokens>
    <token id="1">Auf</token>
    <token id="2">Eis</token>
    <token id="3">gelegt</token>
    <token id="4">Dagmar</token
      >
    <token id="5">Ziegler</token
      >
    <token id="6">sitzt</token>
    <token id="7">in</token>
    <token id="8">der</token>
    <token id="9">Schuldenfalle</
      token>
    <token id="10">.</token>
    <token id="11">Auf</token>
    <token id="12">Grund</token
      >
    <token id="13">der</token>
    <token id="14">dramatischen<
      /token>
    <token id="15">Kassenlage</
      token>
    <token id="16">in</token>
    <token id="17">Brandenburg<
      /token>
    <token id="18">hat</token>
    <token id="19">sie</token>
    <token id="20">jetzt</token>
    <token id="21">eine</token>
    <token id="22">seit</token>
    <token id="23">mehr</token>
    <token id="24">als</token>
    <token id="25">einem</token
      >
    <token id="26">Jahr</token>
    <token id="27">erarbeitete</
      token>
    <token id="28">
      Kabinettsvorlage</token>
    <token id="29">überraschend<
      /token>
    <token id="30">auf</token>
    <token id="31">Eis</token>
    <token id="32">gelegt</token
      >
    <token id="33">und</token>
    <token id="34">vorgeschlagen
      </token>
    <token id="35">,</token>
    <token id="36">erst</token>
    <token id="37">2003</token>
    <token id="38">darüber</
      token>
    <token id="39">zu</token>
    <token id="40">entscheiden</
      token>
    <token id="41">.</token>
    <token id="42">Überraschend
      </token>
    <token id="43">,</token>
    <token id="44">weil</token>
    <token id="45">das</token>
    <token id="46">Finanz-</
      token>
    <token id="47">und</token>
    <token id="48">das</token>
    <token id="49">
      Bildungsressort</token>
    <token id="50">das</token>
    <token id="51">
      Lehrerpersonalkonzept</
      token>
    <token id="52">gemeinsam</
      token>
    <token id="53">entwickelt</
      token>
    <token id="54">hatten</token
      >
```

```
<token id="55">.</token>
<token id="56">Der</token>
<token id="57">Rückzieher</
    token>
<token id="58">der</token>
<token id="59">
    Finanzministerin</token>
<token id="60">ist</token>
<token id="61">aber</token>
<token id="62">verständlich</
    token>
<token id="63">.</token>
<token id="64">Es</token>
<token id="65">dürfte</token
    >
<token id="66">derzeit</token
    >
<token id="67">schwer</token
    >
<token id="68">zu</token>
<token id="69">vermitteln</
    token>
<token id="70">sein</token>
<token id="71">,</token>
<token id="72">weshalb</
    token>
<token id="73">ein</token>
<token id="74">Ressort</
    token>
<token id="75">pauschal</
    token>
<token id="76">von</token>
<token id="77">künftigen</
    token>
<token id="78">Einsparungen
    </token>
<token id="79">ausgenommen
    </token>
<token id="80">werden</
    token>
<token id="81">soll</token>
<token id="82">auf</token>
<token id="83">Kosten</token
    >
<token id="84">der</token>
<token id="85">anderen</
    token>
```

```
<token id="86">.</token>
<token id="87">Reiches</
    token>
<token id="88">
    Ministerkollegen</token>
<token id="89">werden</
    token>
<token id="90">mit</token>
<token id="91">Argusaugen</
    token>
<token id="92">darüber</
    token>
<token id="93">wachen</
    token>
<token id="94">,</token>
<token id="95">dass</token>
<token id="96">das</token>
<token id="97">Konzept</
    token>
<token id="98">wasserdicht</
    token>
<token id="99">ist</token>
<token id="100">.</token>
<token id="101">Tatsächlich</
    token>
<token id="102">gibt</token>
<token id="103">es</token>
<token id="104">noch</token
    >
<token id="105">etliche</
    token>
<token id="106">offene</token
    >
<token id="107">Fragen</
    token>
<token id="108">.</token>
<token id="109">So</token>
<token id="110">ist</token>
<token id="111">etwa</token
    >
<token id="112">unklar</
    token>
<token id="113">,</token>
<token id="114">wer</token>
<token id="115">Abfindungen
    </token>
<token id="116">erhalten</
```

```
                                              <token id="147">künftig</
token>                                           token>
<token id="117">soll</token>                 <token id="148">zu</token>
<token id="118">,</token>                    <token id="149">wenig</token
<token id="119">oder</token                       >
     >                                       <token id="150">Arbeit</
<token id="120">was</token>                       token>
<token id="121">passiert</                   <token id="151">für</token>
     token>                                  <token id="152">zu</token>
<token id="122">,</token>                    <token id="153">viele</token
<token id="123">wenn</token                        >
     >                                       <token id="154">Pädagogen</
<token id="124">zu</token>                        token>
<token id="125">wenig</token                 <token id="155">.</token>
     >                                       <token id="156">Und</token
<token id="126">Lehrer</                           >
     token>                                  <token id="157">die</token>
<token id="127">die</token>                  <token id="158">Zeit</token>
<token id="128">Angebote</                   <token id="159">drängt</
     token>                                       token>
<token id="129">des</token>                  <token id="160">.</token>
<token id="130">vorzeitigen</               <token id="161">Der</token>
     token>                                  <token id="162">große</token
<token id="131">Ausstiegs</                        >
     token>                                  <token id="163">Einbruch</
<token id="132">nutzen</                          token>
     token>                                  <token id="164">der</token>
<token id="133">.</token>                    <token id="165">Schülerzahlen
<token id="134">Dennoch</                          </token>
     token>                                  <token id="166">an</token>
<token id="135">gibt</token>                 <token id="167">den</token>
<token id="136">es</token>                   <token id="168">weiterfü
<token id="137">zu</token>                        hrenden</token>
<token id="138">Reiches</                    <token id="169">Schulen</
     token>                                       token>
<token id="139">                             <token id="170">beginnt</
     Personalpapier</token>                       token>
<token id="140">eigentlich</               <token id="171">bereits</
     token>                                       token>
<token id="141">keine</token                <token id="172">im</token>
     >                                       <token id="173">Herbst</
<token id="142">Alternative</                     token>
     token>                                  <token id="174">2003</token
<token id="143">.</token>                          >
<token id="144">Das</token>                  <token id="175">.</token>
<token id="145">Land</token                 <token id="176">Die</token>
     >                                       <token id="177">Regierung</
<token id="146">hat</token>
```

```
      token>
<token id="178">muss</token
    >
<token id="179">sich</token>
<token id="180">entscheiden<
    /token>
<token id="181">,</token>
<token id="182">und</token>
<token id="183">zwar</token
    >
<token id="184">schnell</
    token>
<token id="185">.</token>
<token id="186">Entweder</
    token>
<token id="187">sparen</
    token>
<token id="188">um</token>
<token id="189">jeden</token
    >
<token id="190">Preis</token
    >
<token id="191">oder</token
    >
<token id="192">Priorität</
    token>
<token id="193">für</token>
<token id="194">die</token>
<token id="195">Bildung</
    token>
<token id="196">.</token>
</tokens>
<relations>
  <relation relation_id="1"
  pdtb3_sense="Contingency.
    Cause.Reason"
  type="explicit">
   <connective_tokens>
    <connective_token id="11"
    token="Auf"/>
    <connective_token id="12"
    token="Grund"/>
   </connective_tokens>
  <int_arg_tokens>
    <int_arg_token id="13"
    token="der"/>
    <int_arg_token id="14"
    token="dramatischen"/>
    <int_arg_token id="15"
    token="Kassenlage"/>
    <int_arg_token id="16"
    token="in"/>
    <int_arg_token id="17"
    token="Brandenburg"/>
  </int_arg_tokens>
  <ext_arg_tokens>
    <ext_arg_token id="18"
    token="hat"/>
    <ext_arg_token id="19"
    token="sie"/>
    <ext_arg_token id="20"
    token="jetzt"/>
    <ext_arg_token id="21"
    token="eine"/>
    <ext_arg_token id="22"
    token="seit"/>
    <ext_arg_token id="23"
    token="mehr"/>
    <ext_arg_token id="24"
    token="als"/>
    <ext_arg_token id="25"
    token="einem"/>
    <ext_arg_token id="26"
    token="Jahr"/>
    <ext_arg_token id="27"
    token="erarbeitete"/>
    <ext_arg_token id="28"
    token="Kabinettsvorlage"/
      >
    <ext_arg_token id="29"
    token="überraschend"/>
    <ext_arg_token id="30"
    token="auf"/>
    <ext_arg_token id="31"
    token="Eis"/>
    <ext_arg_token id="32"
    token="gelegt"/>
  </ext_arg_tokens>
</relation>
<relation relation_id="2"
pdtb3_sense="Expansion.
    Conjunction"
type="explicit">
  <connective_tokens>
```

121

```
        <connective_token id="33"
    token="und"/>
  </connective_tokens>
  <ext_arg_tokens>
        <ext_arg_token id="18"
    token="hat"/>
        <ext_arg_token id="19"
    token="sie"/>
        <ext_arg_token id="20"
    token="jetzt"/>
        <ext_arg_token id="21"
    token="eine"/>
        <ext_arg_token id="22"
    token="seit"/>
        <ext_arg_token id="23"
    token="mehr"/>
        <ext_arg_token id="24"
    token="als"/>
        <ext_arg_token id="25"
    token="einem"/>
        <ext_arg_token id="26"
    token="Jahr"/>
        <ext_arg_token id="27"
    token="erarbeitete"/>
        <ext_arg_token id="28"
    token="Kabinettsvorlage"/
        >
        <ext_arg_token id="29"
    token="überraschend"/>
        <ext_arg_token id="30"
    token="auf"/>
        <ext_arg_token id="31"
    token="Eis"/>
        <ext_arg_token id="32"
    token="gelegt"/>
  </ext_arg_tokens>
  <int_arg_tokens>
        <int_arg_token id="34"
    token="vorgeschlagen"/>
        <int_arg_token id="35"
    token=","/>
        <int_arg_token id="36"
    token="erst"/>
        <int_arg_token id="37"
    token="2003"/>
        <int_arg_token id="38"
    token="darüber"/>
```

```
        <int_arg_token id="39"
    token="zu"/>
        <int_arg_token id="40"
    token="entscheiden"/>
        <int_arg_token id="41"
    token="."/>
  </int_arg_tokens>
</relation>
<relation relation_id="4"
  pdtb3_sense="Contingency.
      Cause.Reason"
  type="explicit">
  <connective_tokens>
        <connective_token id="44"
    token="weil"/>
  </connective_tokens>
  <ext_arg_tokens>
        <ext_arg_token id="42"
    token="Überraschend"/>
        <ext_arg_token id="43"
    token=","/>
  </ext_arg_tokens>
  <int_arg_tokens>
        <int_arg_token id="45"
    token="das"/>
        <int_arg_token id="46"
    token="Finanz-"/>
        <int_arg_token id="47"
    token="und"/>
        <int_arg_token id="48"
    token="das"/>
        <int_arg_token id="49"
    token="Bildungsressort"/>
        <int_arg_token id="50"
    token="das"/>
        <int_arg_token id="51"
    token="
        Lehrerpersonalkonzept"
        />
        <int_arg_token id="52"
    token="gemeinsam"/>
        <int_arg_token id="53"
    token="entwickelt"/>
        <int_arg_token id="54"
    token="hatten"/>
        <int_arg_token id="55"
    token="."/>
```

```
        </int_arg_tokens>
  </relation>
  <relation relation_id="5"
   pdtb3_sense="Comparison.
        Concession.Arg2-as-
        denier"
   type="explicit">
    <connective_tokens>
      <connective_token id="61"
      token="aber"/>
    </connective_tokens>
    <ext_arg_tokens>
      <ext_arg_token id="42"
      token="Überraschend"/>
      <ext_arg_token id="43"
      token=","/>
      <ext_arg_token id="44"
      token="weil"/>
      <ext_arg_token id="45"
      token="das"/>
      <ext_arg_token id="46"
      token="Finanz-"/>
      <ext_arg_token id="47"
      token="und"/>
      <ext_arg_token id="48"
      token="das"/>
      <ext_arg_token id="49"
      token="Bildungsressort"/>
      <ext_arg_token id="50"
      token="das"/>
      <ext_arg_token id="51"
      token="
          Lehrerpersonalkonzept"
          />
      <ext_arg_token id="52"
      token="gemeinsam"/>
      <ext_arg_token id="53"
      token="entwickelt"/>
      <ext_arg_token id="54"
      token="hatten"/>
      <ext_arg_token id="55"
      token="."/>
    </ext_arg_tokens>
    <int_arg_tokens>
      <int_arg_token id="56"
      token="Der"/>
      <int_arg_token id="57"
```
```
      token="Rückzieher"/>
      <int_arg_token id="58"
      token="der"/>
      <int_arg_token id="59"
      token="Finanzministerin"/
          >
      <int_arg_token id="60"
      token="ist"/>
      <int_arg_token id="62"
      token="verständlich"/>
      <int_arg_token id="63"
      token="."/>
    </int_arg_tokens>
  </relation>
  <relation relation_id="7"
   pdtb3_sense="Expansion.
        Disjunction"
   type="explicit">
    <connective_tokens>
      <connective_token id="119
          "
      token="oder"/>
    </connective_tokens>
    <ext_arg_tokens>
      <ext_arg_token id="114"
      token="wer"/>
      <ext_arg_token id="115"
      token="Abfindungen"/>
      <ext_arg_token id="116"
      token="erhalten"/>
      <ext_arg_token id="117"
      token="soll"/>
      <ext_arg_token id="118"
      token=","/>
    </ext_arg_tokens>
    <int_arg_tokens>
      <int_arg_token id="120"
      token="was"/>
      <int_arg_token id="121"
      token="passiert"/>
      <int_arg_token id="122"
      token=","/>
      <int_arg_token id="123"
      token="wenn"/>
      <int_arg_token id="124"
      token="zu"/>
      <int_arg_token id="125"
```

```xml
        token="wenig"/>
        <int_arg_token id="126"
        token="Lehrer"/>
        <int_arg_token id="127"
        token="die"/>
        <int_arg_token id="128"
        token="Angebote"/>
        <int_arg_token id="129"
        token="des"/>
        <int_arg_token id="130"
        token="vorzeitigen"/>
        <int_arg_token id="131"
        token="Ausstiegs"/>
        <int_arg_token id="132"
        token="nutzen"/>
        <int_arg_token id="133"
        token="."/>
      </int_arg_tokens>
    </relation>
    <relation relation_id="8"
    pdtb3_sense="Contingency.
        Condition.Arg2-as-cond"
    type="explicit">
      <connective_tokens>
        <connective_token id="123
        "
        token="wenn"/>
      </connective_tokens>
      <ext_arg_tokens>
        <ext_arg_token id="120"
        token="was"/>
        <ext_arg_token id="121"
        token="passiert"/>
        <ext_arg_token id="122"
        token=","/>
      </ext_arg_tokens>
      <int_arg_tokens>
        <int_arg_token id="124"
        token="zu"/>
        <int_arg_token id="125"
        token="wenig"/>
        <int_arg_token id="126"
        token="Lehrer"/>
        <int_arg_token id="127"
        token="die"/>
        <int_arg_token id="128"
        token="Angebote"/>
        <int_arg_token id="129"
        token="des"/>
        <int_arg_token id="130"
        token="vorzeitigen"/>
        <int_arg_token id="131"
        token="Ausstiegs"/>
        <int_arg_token id="132"
        token="nutzen"/>
        <int_arg_token id="133"
        token="."/>
      </int_arg_tokens>
    </relation>
    <relation relation_id="9"
    pdtb3_sense="Comparison.
        Concession.Arg2-as-
        denier"
    type="explicit">
      <connective_tokens>
        <connective_token id="134
        "
        token="Dennoch"/>
      </connective_tokens>
      <ext_arg_tokens>
        <ext_arg_token id="109"
        token="So"/>
        <ext_arg_token id="110"
        token="ist"/>
        <ext_arg_token id="111"
        token="etwa"/>
        <ext_arg_token id="112"
        token="unklar"/>
        <ext_arg_token id="113"
        token=","/>
        <ext_arg_token id="114"
        token="wer"/>
        <ext_arg_token id="115"
        token="Abfindungen"/>
        <ext_arg_token id="116"
        token="erhalten"/>
        <ext_arg_token id="117"
        token="soll"/>
        <ext_arg_token id="118"
        token=","/>
        <ext_arg_token id="119"
        token="oder"/>
        <ext_arg_token id="120"
        token="was"/>
```

```
<ext_arg_token id="121"                </relation>
token="passiert"/>                    <relation relation_id="10"
<ext_arg_token id="122"                pdtb3_sense="Expansion.
token=","/>                               Conjunction"
<ext_arg_token id="123"               type="explicit">
token="wenn"/>                         <connective_tokens>
<ext_arg_token id="124"                 <connective_token id="156
token="zu"/>                                 "
<ext_arg_token id="125"                 token="Und"/>
token="wenig"/>                        </connective_tokens>
<ext_arg_token id="126"                <ext_arg_tokens>
token="Lehrer"/>                        <ext_arg_token id="144"
<ext_arg_token id="127"                 token="Das"/>
token="die"/>                           <ext_arg_token id="145"
<ext_arg_token id="128"                 token="Land"/>
token="Angebote"/>                      <ext_arg_token id="146"
<ext_arg_token id="129"                 token="hat"/>
token="des"/>                           <ext_arg_token id="147"
<ext_arg_token id="130"                 token="künftig"/>
token="vorzeitigen"/>                   <ext_arg_token id="148"
<ext_arg_token id="131"                 token="zu"/>
token="Ausstiegs"/>                     <ext_arg_token id="149"
<ext_arg_token id="132"                 token="wenig"/>
token="nutzen"/>                        <ext_arg_token id="150"
<ext_arg_token id="133"                 token="Arbeit"/>
token="."/>                             <ext_arg_token id="151"
</ext_arg_tokens>                        token="für"/>
<int_arg_tokens>                        <ext_arg_token id="152"
<int_arg_token id="135"                 token="zu"/>
token="gibt"/>                          <ext_arg_token id="153"
<int_arg_token id="136"                 token="viele"/>
token="es"/>                            <ext_arg_token id="154"
<int_arg_token id="137"                 token="Pädagogen"/>
token="zu"/>                            <ext_arg_token id="155"
<int_arg_token id="138"                 token="."/>
token="Reiches"/>                      </ext_arg_tokens>
<int_arg_token id="139"                <int_arg_tokens>
token="Personalpapier"/>                <int_arg_token id="157"
<int_arg_token id="140"                 token="die"/>
token="eigentlich"/>                    <int_arg_token id="158"
<int_arg_token id="141"                 token="Zeit"/>
token="keine"/>                         <int_arg_token id="159"
<int_arg_token id="142"                 token="drängt"/>
token="Alternative"/>                   <int_arg_token id="160"
<int_arg_token id="143"                 token="."/>
token="."/>                            </int_arg_tokens>
</int_arg_tokens>                      </relation>
```

```
<relation relation_id="11"
pdtb3_sense="Expansion.
    Disjunction"
type="explicit">
  <connective_tokens>
    <connective_token id="186
    "
    token="Entweder"/>
    <connective_token id="191
    "
    token="oder"/>
  </connective_tokens>
  <int_arg_tokens>
    <int_arg_token id="192"
    token="Priorität"/>
    <int_arg_token id="193"
    token="für"/>
    <int_arg_token id="194"
    token="die"/>
    <int_arg_token id="195"
    token="Bildung"/>
    <int_arg_token id="196"
    token="."/>
  </int_arg_tokens>
  <ext_arg_tokens>
    <ext_arg_token id="186"
    token="Entweder"/>
    <ext_arg_token id="187"
    token="sparen"/>
    <ext_arg_token id="188"
    token="um"/>
    <ext_arg_token id="189"
    token="jeden"/>
    <ext_arg_token id="190"
    token="Preis"/>
  </ext_arg_tokens>
</relation>
<relation relation_id="12"
type="EntRel">
  <connective_tokens>
    <implicit_connective/>
  </connective_tokens>
  <ext_arg_tokens>
    <ext_arg_token id="4"
    token="Dagmar"/>
    <ext_arg_token id="5"
    token="Ziegler"/>
```

```
    <ext_arg_token id="6"
    token="sitzt"/>
    <ext_arg_token id="7"
    token="in"/>
    <ext_arg_token id="8"
    token="der"/>
    <ext_arg_token id="9"
    token="Schuldenfalle"/>
    <ext_arg_token id="10"
    token="."/>
  </ext_arg_tokens>
<int_arg_tokens>
    <int_arg_token id="11"
    token="Auf"/>
    <int_arg_token id="12"
    token="Grund"/>
    <int_arg_token id="13"
    token="der"/>
    <int_arg_token id="14"
    token="dramatischen"/>
    <int_arg_token id="15"
    token="Kassenlage"/>
    <int_arg_token id="16"
    token="in"/>
    <int_arg_token id="17"
    token="Brandenburg"/>
    <int_arg_token id="18"
    token="hat"/>
    <int_arg_token id="19"
    token="sie"/>
    <int_arg_token id="20"
    token="jetzt"/>
    <int_arg_token id="21"
    token="eine"/>
    <int_arg_token id="22"
    token="seit"/>
    <int_arg_token id="23"
    token="mehr"/>
    <int_arg_token id="24"
    token="als"/>
    <int_arg_token id="25"
    token="einem"/>
    <int_arg_token id="26"
    token="Jahr"/>
    <int_arg_token id="27"
    token="erarbeitete"/>
    <int_arg_token id="28"
```

```
token="Kabinettsvorlage"/
    >
<int_arg_token id="29"
token="überraschend"/>
<int_arg_token id="30"
token="auf"/>
<int_arg_token id="31"
token="Eis"/>
<int_arg_token id="32"
token="gelegt"/>
<int_arg_token id="33"
token="und"/>
<int_arg_token id="34"
token="vorgeschlagen"/>
<int_arg_token id="35"
token=","/>
<int_arg_token id="36"
token="erst"/>
<int_arg_token id="37"
token="2003"/>
<int_arg_token id="38"
token="darüber"/>
<int_arg_token id="39"
token="zu"/>
<int_arg_token id="40"
token="entscheiden"/>
<int_arg_token id="41"
token="."/>
</int_arg_tokens>
</relation>
<relation relation_id="13"
pdtb3_sense="Comparison.
    Concession.Arg2—as—
    denier"
type="implicit">
<connective_tokens>
  <implicit_connective>
      jedoch</
      implicit_connective>
</connective_tokens>
<ext_arg_tokens>
  <ext_arg_token id="11"
token="Auf"/>
  <ext_arg_token id="12"
token="Grund"/>
  <ext_arg_token id="13"
token="der"/>
```

```
<ext_arg_token id="14"
token="dramatischen"/>
<ext_arg_token id="15"
token="Kassenlage"/>
<ext_arg_token id="16"
token="in"/>
<ext_arg_token id="17"
token="Brandenburg"/>
<ext_arg_token id="18"
token="hat"/>
<ext_arg_token id="19"
token="sie"/>
<ext_arg_token id="20"
token="jetzt"/>
<ext_arg_token id="21"
token="eine"/>
<ext_arg_token id="22"
token="seit"/>
<ext_arg_token id="23"
token="mehr"/>
<ext_arg_token id="24"
token="als"/>
<ext_arg_token id="25"
token="einem"/>
<ext_arg_token id="26"
token="Jahr"/>
<ext_arg_token id="27"
token="erarbeitete"/>
<ext_arg_token id="28"
token="Kabinettsvorlage"/
    >
<ext_arg_token id="29"
token="überraschend"/>
<ext_arg_token id="30"
token="auf"/>
<ext_arg_token id="31"
token="Eis"/>
<ext_arg_token id="32"
token="gelegt"/>
<ext_arg_token id="33"
token="und"/>
<ext_arg_token id="34"
token="vorgeschlagen"/>
<ext_arg_token id="35"
token=","/>
<ext_arg_token id="36"
token="erst"/>
```

```xml
        <ext_arg_token id="37"
token="2003"/>
        <ext_arg_token id="38"
token="darüber"/>
        <ext_arg_token id="39"
token="zu"/>
        <ext_arg_token id="40"
token="entscheiden"/>
        <ext_arg_token id="41"
token="."/>
      </ext_arg_tokens>
      <int_arg_tokens>
        <int_arg_token id="42"
token="Überraschend"/>
        <int_arg_token id="43"
token=","/>
        <int_arg_token id="44"
token="weil"/>
        <int_arg_token id="45"
token="das"/>
        <int_arg_token id="46"
token="Finanz—"/>
        <int_arg_token id="47"
token="und"/>
        <int_arg_token id="48"
token="das"/>
        <int_arg_token id="49"
token="Bildungsressort"/>
        <int_arg_token id="50"
token="das"/>
        <int_arg_token id="51"
token="
        Lehrerpersonalkonzept"
/>
        <int_arg_token id="52"
token="gemeinsam"/>
        <int_arg_token id="53"
token="entwickelt"/>
        <int_arg_token id="54"
token="hatten"/>
        <int_arg_token id="55"
token="."/>
      </int_arg_tokens>
    </relation>
<relation relation_id="14"
  pdtb3_sense="Contingency.
    Cause.Reason"
type="implicit">
    <connective_tokens>
      <implicit_connective>weil<
        /implicit_connective>
    </connective_tokens>
    <ext_arg_tokens>
      <ext_arg_token id="56"
token="Der"/>
      <ext_arg_token id="57"
token="Rückzieher"/>
      <ext_arg_token id="58"
token="der"/>
      <ext_arg_token id="59"
token="Finanzministerin"/
    >
      <ext_arg_token id="60"
token="ist"/>
      <ext_arg_token id="61"
token="aber"/>
      <ext_arg_token id="62"
token="verständlich"/>
      <ext_arg_token id="63"
token="."/>
    </ext_arg_tokens>
    <int_arg_tokens>
      <int_arg_token id="64"
token="Es"/>
      <int_arg_token id="65"
token="dürfte"/>
      <int_arg_token id="66"
token="derzeit"/>
      <int_arg_token id="67"
token="schwer"/>
      <int_arg_token id="68"
token="zu"/>
      <int_arg_token id="69"
token="vermitteln"/>
      <int_arg_token id="70"
token="sein"/>
      <int_arg_token id="71"
token=","/>
      <int_arg_token id="72"
token="weshalb"/>
      <int_arg_token id="73"
token="ein"/>
      <int_arg_token id="74"
token="Ressort"/>
```

```
  <int_arg_token id="75"                    token="vermitteln"/>
  token="pauschal"/>                      <ext_arg_token id="70"
  <int_arg_token id="76"                    token="sein"/>
  token="von"/>                           <ext_arg_token id="71"
  <int_arg_token id="77"                    token=","/>
  token="künftigen"/>                     <ext_arg_token id="72"
  <int_arg_token id="78"                    token="weshalb"/>
  token="Einsparungen"/>                  <ext_arg_token id="73"
  <int_arg_token id="79"                    token="ein"/>
  token="ausgenommen"/>                   <ext_arg_token id="74"
  <int_arg_token id="80"                    token="Ressort"/>
  token="werden"/>                        <ext_arg_token id="75"
  <int_arg_token id="81"                    token="pauschal"/>
  token="soll"/>                          <ext_arg_token id="76"
  <int_arg_token id="82"                    token="von"/>
  token="auf"/>                           <ext_arg_token id="77"
  <int_arg_token id="83"                    token="künftigen"/>
  token="Kosten"/>                        <ext_arg_token id="78"
  <int_arg_token id="84"                    token="Einsparungen"/>
  token="der"/>                           <ext_arg_token id="79"
  <int_arg_token id="85"                    token="ausgenommen"/>
  token="anderen"/>                       <ext_arg_token id="80"
  <int_arg_token id="86"                    token="werden"/>
  token="."/>                             <ext_arg_token id="81"
  </int_arg_tokens>                         token="soll"/>
</relation>                               <ext_arg_token id="82"
<relation relation_id="15"                  token="auf"/>
 pdtb3_sense="Contingency.              <ext_arg_token id="83"
    Cause.Result"                         token="Kosten"/>
 type="implicit">                       <ext_arg_token id="84"
  <connective_tokens>                      token="der"/>
    <implicit_connective>                <ext_arg_token id="85"
        deshalb</                          token="anderen"/>
        implicit_connective>             <ext_arg_token id="86"
  </connective_tokens>                     token="."/>
  <ext_arg_tokens>                       </ext_arg_tokens>
    <ext_arg_token id="64"               <int_arg_tokens>
    token="Es"/>                           <int_arg_token id="87"
    <ext_arg_token id="65"                 token="Reiches"/>
    token="dürfte"/>                      <int_arg_token id="88"
    <ext_arg_token id="66"                 token="Ministerkollegen"/>
    token="derzeit"/>                    <int_arg_token id="89"
    <ext_arg_token id="67"                 token="werden"/>
    token="schwer"/>                     <int_arg_token id="90"
    <ext_arg_token id="68"                 token="mit"/>
    token="zu"/>                         <int_arg_token id="91"
    <ext_arg_token id="69"                 token="Argusaugen"/>
```

```
        <int_arg_token id="92"
        token="darüber"/>
        <int_arg_token id="93"
        token="wachen"/>
        <int_arg_token id="94"
        token=","/>
        <int_arg_token id="95"
        token="dass"/>
        <int_arg_token id="96"
        token="das"/>
        <int_arg_token id="97"
        token="Konzept"/>
        <int_arg_token id="98"
        token="wasserdicht"/>
        <int_arg_token id="99"
        token="ist"/>
        <int_arg_token id="100"
        token="."/>
      </int_arg_tokens>
  </relation>
  <relation relation_id="16"
  pdtb3_sense="Contingency.
      Cause.Reason"
  type="implicit">
    <connective_tokens>
      <implicit_connective>weil<
          /implicit_connective>
    </connective_tokens>
    <ext_arg_tokens>
        <ext_arg_token id="87"
        token="Reiches"/>
        <ext_arg_token id="88"
        token="Ministerkollegen"/>
        <ext_arg_token id="89"
        token="werden"/>
        <ext_arg_token id="90"
        token="mit"/>
        <ext_arg_token id="91"
        token="Argusaugen"/>
        <ext_arg_token id="92"
        token="darüber"/>
        <ext_arg_token id="93"
        token="wachen"/>
        <ext_arg_token id="94"
        token=","/>
        <ext_arg_token id="95"
        token="dass"/>
```

```
        <ext_arg_token id="96"
        token="das"/>
        <ext_arg_token id="97"
        token="Konzept"/>
        <ext_arg_token id="98"
        token="wasserdicht"/>
        <ext_arg_token id="99"
        token="ist"/>
        <ext_arg_token id="100"
        token="."/>
      </ext_arg_tokens>
    <int_arg_tokens>
        <int_arg_token id="101"
        token="Tatsächlich"/>
        <int_arg_token id="102"
        token="gibt"/>
        <int_arg_token id="103"
        token="es"/>
        <int_arg_token id="104"
        token="noch"/>
        <int_arg_token id="105"
        token="etliche"/>
        <int_arg_token id="106"
        token="offene"/>
        <int_arg_token id="107"
        token="Fragen"/>
        <int_arg_token id="108"
        token="."/>
      </int_arg_tokens>
  </relation>
  <relation relation_id="17"
  pdtb3_sense="Expansion.
      Instantiation.Arg2-as-
      instance"
  type="AltLex">
    <connective_tokens>
      <implicit_connective/>
    </connective_tokens>
    <ext_arg_tokens>
        <ext_arg_token id="101"
        token="Tatsächlich"/>
        <ext_arg_token id="102"
        token="gibt"/>
        <ext_arg_token id="103"
        token="es"/>
        <ext_arg_token id="104"
        token="noch"/>
```

```xml
<ext_arg_token id="105"
token="etliche"/>
<ext_arg_token id="106"
token="offene"/>
<ext_arg_token id="107"
token="Fragen"/>
<ext_arg_token id="108"
token="."/>
</ext_arg_tokens>
<int_arg_tokens>
<int_arg_token id="109"
token="So"/>
<int_arg_token id="110"
token="ist"/>
<int_arg_token id="111"
token="etwa"/>
<int_arg_token id="112"
token="unklar"/>
<int_arg_token id="113"
token=","/>
<int_arg_token id="114"
token="wer"/>
<int_arg_token id="115"
token="Abfindungen"/>
<int_arg_token id="116"
token="erhalten"/>
<int_arg_token id="117"
token="soll"/>
<int_arg_token id="118"
token=","/>
<int_arg_token id="119"
token="oder"/>
<int_arg_token id="120"
token="was"/>
<int_arg_token id="121"
token="passiert"/>
<int_arg_token id="122"
token=","/>
<int_arg_token id="123"
token="wenn"/>
<int_arg_token id="124"
token="zu"/>
<int_arg_token id="125"
token="wenig"/>
<int_arg_token id="126"
token="Lehrer"/>
<int_arg_token id="127"
```

```xml
token="die"/>
<int_arg_token id="128"
token="Angebote"/>
<int_arg_token id="129"
token="des"/>
<int_arg_token id="130"
token="vorzeitigen"/>
<int_arg_token id="131"
token="Ausstiegs"/>
<int_arg_token id="132"
token="nutzen"/>
<int_arg_token id="133"
token="."/>
</int_arg_tokens>
</relation>
<relation relation_id="18"
pdtb3_sense="Contingency.
    Cause.Reason"
type="implicit">
<connective_tokens>
<implicit_connective>weil<
    /implicit_connective>
</connective_tokens>
<ext_arg_tokens>
<ext_arg_token id="134"
token="Dennoch"/>
<ext_arg_token id="135"
token="gibt"/>
<ext_arg_token id="136"
token="es"/>
<ext_arg_token id="137"
token="zu"/>
<ext_arg_token id="138"
token="Reiches"/>
<ext_arg_token id="139"
token="Personalpapier"/>
<ext_arg_token id="140"
token="eigentlich"/>
<ext_arg_token id="141"
token="keine"/>
<ext_arg_token id="142"
token="Alternative"/>
<ext_arg_token id="143"
token="."/>
</ext_arg_tokens>
<int_arg_tokens>
<int_arg_token id="144"
```

```
        token="Das"/>
      <int_arg_token id="145"
        token="Land"/>
      <int_arg_token id="146"
        token="hat"/>
      <int_arg_token id="147"
        token="künftig"/>
      <int_arg_token id="148"
        token="zu"/>
      <int_arg_token id="149"
        token="wenig"/>
      <int_arg_token id="150"
        token="Arbeit"/>
      <int_arg_token id="151"
        token="für"/>
      <int_arg_token id="152"
        token="zu"/>
      <int_arg_token id="153"
        token="viele"/>
      <int_arg_token id="154"
        token="Pädagogen"/>
      <int_arg_token id="155"
        token="."/>
    </int_arg_tokens>
  </relation>
<relation relation_id="19"
  pdtb3_sense="Contingency.
      Cause.Reason"
type="implicit">
  <connective_tokens>
    <implicit_connective>weil<
        /implicit_connective>
  </connective_tokens>
  <ext_arg_tokens>
    <ext_arg_token id="156"
      token="Und"/>
    <ext_arg_token id="157"
      token="die"/>
    <ext_arg_token id="158"
      token="Zeit"/>
    <ext_arg_token id="159"
      token="drängt"/>
    <ext_arg_token id="160"
      token="."/>
  </ext_arg_tokens>
  <int_arg_tokens>
    <int_arg_token id="161"
```

```
        token="Der"/>
      <int_arg_token id="162"
        token="große"/>
      <int_arg_token id="163"
        token="Einbruch"/>
      <int_arg_token id="164"
        token="der"/>
      <int_arg_token id="165"
        token="Schülerzahlen"/>
      <int_arg_token id="166"
        token="an"/>
      <int_arg_token id="167"
        token="den"/>
      <int_arg_token id="168"
        token="weiterführenden"/>
      <int_arg_token id="169"
        token="Schulen"/>
      <int_arg_token id="170"
        token="beginnt"/>
      <int_arg_token id="171"
        token="bereits"/>
      <int_arg_token id="172"
        token="im"/>
      <int_arg_token id="173"
        token="Herbst"/>
      <int_arg_token id="174"
        token="2003"/>
      <int_arg_token id="175"
        token="."/>
    </int_arg_tokens>
  </relation>
<relation relation_id="20"
  pdtb3_sense="Contingency.
      Cause.Result"
type="implicit">
  <connective_tokens>
    <implicit_connective>
        deshalb</
        implicit_connective>
  </connective_tokens>
  <ext_arg_tokens>
    <ext_arg_token id="161"
      token="Der"/>
    <ext_arg_token id="162"
      token="große"/>
    <ext_arg_token id="163"
      token="Einbruch"/>
```

```
<ext_arg_token id="164"
token="der"/>
<ext_arg_token id="165"
token="Schülerzahlen"/>
<ext_arg_token id="166"
token="an"/>
<ext_arg_token id="167"
token="den"/>
<ext_arg_token id="168"
token="weiterführenden"/>
<ext_arg_token id="169"
token="Schulen"/>
<ext_arg_token id="170"
token="beginnt"/>
<ext_arg_token id="171"
token="bereits"/>
<ext_arg_token id="172"
token="im"/>
<ext_arg_token id="173"
token="Herbst"/>
<ext_arg_token id="174"
token="2003"/>
<ext_arg_token id="175"
token="."/>
</ext_arg_tokens>
<int_arg_tokens>
  <int_arg_token id="176"
token="Die"/>
  <int_arg_token id="177"
token="Regierung"/>
  <int_arg_token id="178"
token="muss"/>
  <int_arg_token id="179"
token="sich"/>
  <int_arg_token id="180"
token="entscheiden"/>
  <int_arg_token id="181"
token=","/>
  <int_arg_token id="182"
token="und"/>
  <int_arg_token id="183"
token="zwar"/>
  <int_arg_token id="184"
token="schnell"/>
  <int_arg_token id="185"
token="."/>
</int_arg_tokens>

</relation>
<relation relation_id="21"
 type="NoRel">
  <connective_tokens>
    <implicit_connective/>
  </connective_tokens>
  <ext_arg_tokens>
    <ext_arg_token id="176"
token="Die"/>
    <ext_arg_token id="177"
token="Regierung"/>
    <ext_arg_token id="178"
token="muss"/>
    <ext_arg_token id="179"
token="sich"/>
    <ext_arg_token id="180"
token="entscheiden"/>
    <ext_arg_token id="181"
token=","/>
    <ext_arg_token id="182"
token="und"/>
    <ext_arg_token id="183"
token="zwar"/>
    <ext_arg_token id="184"
token="schnell"/>
    <ext_arg_token id="185"
token="."/>
  </ext_arg_tokens>
  <int_arg_tokens>
    <int_arg_token id="186"
token="Entweder"/>
    <int_arg_token id="187"
token="sparen"/>
    <int_arg_token id="188"
token="um"/>
    <int_arg_token id="189"
token="jeden"/>
    <int_arg_token id="190"
token="Preis"/>
    <int_arg_token id="191"
token="oder"/>
    <int_arg_token id="192"
token="Priorität"/>
    <int_arg_token id="193"
token="für"/>
    <int_arg_token id="194"
token="die"/>
```

```
<int_arg_token id="195"
token="Bildung"/>
<int_arg_token id="196"
token="."/>
</int_arg_tokens>
```

```
</relation>
</relations>
</discourse>
```

Appendix B

Parser Output

B.1. PDTB-JSON output format

[
{'ID': 1, 'DocID': '06−08−2020_17:29:47', 'Sense': 'Contingency.Cause.Reason',
'Type': 'Explicit', 'Arg1': {'CharacterSpanList': [], 'RawText': '', '
TokenList': []}, 'Arg2': {'CharacterSpanList': [[73, 271]], 'RawText': 'der
dramatischen Kassenlage in Brandenburg hat sie jetzt eine seit mehr als
einem Jahr erarbeitete Kabinettsvorlage überraschend auf Eis gelegt und
vorgeschlagen , erst 2003 darüber zu entscheiden .', 'TokenList': [[73, 76,
14, 1, 2], [77, 89, 15, 1, 3], [90, 100, 16, 1, 4], [101, 103, 17, 1, 5], [104, 115,
18, 1, 6], [116, 119, 19, 1, 7], [120, 123, 20, 1, 8], [124, 129, 21, 1, 9], [130,
134, 22, 1, 10], [135, 139, 23, 1, 11], [140, 144, 24, 1, 12], [145, 148, 25, 1,
13], [149, 154, 26, 1, 14], [155, 159, 27, 1, 15], [160, 171, 28, 1, 16], [172,
188, 29, 1, 17], [189, 201, 30, 1, 18], [202, 205, 31, 1, 19], [206, 209, 32, 1,
20], [210, 216, 33, 1, 21], [217, 220, 34, 1, 22], [221, 234, 35, 1, 23], [235,
236, 36, 1, 24], [237, 241, 37, 1, 25], [242, 246, 38, 1, 26], [247, 254, 39, 1,
27], [255, 257, 40, 1, 28], [258, 269, 41, 1, 29], [270, 271, 42, 1, 30]]}, '
Connective': {'CharacterSpanList': [[63, 72]], 'RawText': 'Auf Grund', '
TokenList': [[63, 66, 12, 1, 0], [67, 72, 13, 1, 1]]}}
{'ID': 2, 'DocID': '06−08−2020_17:29:47', 'Sense': 'Expansion.Conjunction', '
Type': 'Explicit', 'Arg1': {'CharacterSpanList': [[63, 216], [237, 271]], '
RawText': 'Auf Grund der dramatischen Kassenlage in Brandenburg hat
sie jetzt eine seit mehr als einem Jahr erarbeitete Kabinettsvorlage ü
berraschend auf Eis gelegt erst 2003 darüber zu entscheiden .', 'TokenList':
[[63, 66, 12, 1, 0], [67, 72, 13, 1, 1], [73, 76, 14, 1, 2], [77, 89, 15, 1, 3], [90,
100, 16, 1, 4], [101, 103, 17, 1, 5], [104, 115, 18, 1, 6], [116, 119, 19, 1, 7],
[120, 123, 20, 1, 8], [124, 129, 21, 1, 9], [130, 134, 22, 1, 10], [135, 139, 23,
1, 11], [140, 144, 24, 1, 12], [145, 148, 25, 1, 13], [149, 154, 26, 1, 14], [155,
159, 27, 1, 15], [160, 171, 28, 1, 16], [172, 188, 29, 1, 17], [189, 201, 30, 1,
18], [202, 205, 31, 1, 19], [206, 209, 32, 1, 20], [210, 216, 33, 1, 21], [237,
241, 37, 1, 25], [242, 246, 38, 1, 26], [247, 254, 39, 1, 27], [255, 257, 40, 1,

28], [258, 269, 41, 1, 29], [270, 271, 42, 1, 30]]]}, 'Arg2': {'CharacterSpanList': [[221, 236]], 'RawText': 'vorgeschlagen ,', 'TokenList': [[221, 234, 35, 1, 23], [235, 236, 36, 1, 24]]]}, 'Connective': {'CharacterSpanList': [[217, 220]], 'RawText': 'und', 'TokenList': [[217, 220, 34, 1, 22]]]}}}

{'ID': 3, 'DocID': '06−08−2020_17:29:47', 'Sense': 'Contingency.Cause.Reason', 'Type': 'Explicit', 'Arg1': {'CharacterSpanList': [[272, 286]], 'RawText': 'Ü berraschend ,', 'TokenList': [[272, 284, 43, 2, 0], [285, 286, 44, 2, 1]]]}, 'Arg2': {'CharacterSpanList': [[292, 383]], 'RawText': 'das Finanz− und das Bildungsressort das Lehrerpersonalkonzept gemeinsam entwickelt hatten .', 'TokenList': [[292, 295, 46, 2, 3], [296, 303, 47, 2, 4], [304, 307, 48, 2, 5], [308, 311, 49, 2, 6], [312, 327, 50, 2, 7], [328, 331, 51, 2, 8], [332, 353, 52, 2, 9], [354, 363, 53, 2, 10], [364, 374, 54, 2, 11], [375, 381, 55, 2, 12], [382, 383, 56, 2, 13]]]}, 'Connective': {'CharacterSpanList': [[287, 291]], 'RawText': 'weil', 'TokenList': [[287, 291, 45, 2, 2]]]}}}

{'ID': 4, 'DocID': '06−08−2020_17:29:47', 'Sense': 'Comparison.Concession. Arg2−as−denier', 'Type': 'Explicit', 'Arg1': {'CharacterSpanList': [[272, 383]], 'RawText': 'Überraschend , weil das Finanz− und das Bildungsressort das Lehrerpersonalkonzept gemeinsam entwickelt hatten .', 'TokenList': [[272, 284, 43, 2, 0], [285, 286, 44, 2, 1], [287, 291, 45, 2, 2], [292, 295, 46, 2, 3], [296, 303, 47, 2, 4], [304, 307, 48, 2, 5], [308, 311, 49, 2, 6], [312, 327, 50, 2, 7], [328, 331, 51, 2, 8], [332, 353, 52, 2, 9], [354, 363, 53, 2, 10], [364, 374, 54, 2, 11], [375, 381, 55, 2, 12], [382, 383, 56, 2, 13]]]}, 'Arg2': {'CharacterSpanList': [[384, 423], [429, 443]], 'RawText': 'Der Rü ckzieher der Finanzministerin ist verständlich .', 'TokenList': [[384, 387, 57, 3, 0], [388, 398, 58, 3, 1], [399, 402, 59, 3, 2], [403, 419, 60, 3, 3], [420, 423, 61, 3, 4], [429, 441, 63, 3, 6], [442, 443, 64, 3, 7]]]}, 'Connective': {'CharacterSpanList': [[424, 428]], 'RawText': 'aber', 'TokenList': [[424, 428, 62, 3, 5]]]}}}

{'ID': 5, 'DocID': '06−08−2020_17:29:47', 'Sense': 'Expansion.Disjunction', 'Type': 'Explicit', 'Arg1': {'CharacterSpanList': [[743, 795]], 'RawText': 'So ist etwa unklar , wer Abfindungen erhalten soll ,', 'TokenList': [[743, 745, 110, 7, 0], [746, 749, 111, 7, 1], [750, 754, 112, 7, 2], [755, 761, 113, 7, 3], [762, 763, 114, 7, 4], [764, 767, 115, 7, 5], [768, 779, 116, 7, 6], [780, 788, 117, 7, 7], [789, 793, 118, 7, 8], [794, 795, 119, 7, 9]]]}, 'Arg2': {'CharacterSpanList': [[801, 884]], 'RawText': 'was passiert , wenn zu wenig Lehrer die Angebote des vorzeitigen Ausstiegs nutzen .', 'TokenList': [[801, 804, 121, 7, 11], [805, 813, 122, 7, 12], [814, 815, 123, 7, 13], [816, 820, 124, 7, 14], [821, 823, 125, 7, 15], [824, 829, 126, 7, 16], [830, 836, 127, 7, 17], [837, 840, 128, 7, 18], [841, 849, 129, 7, 19], [850, 853, 130, 7, 20], [854, 865, 131, 7, 21], [866, 875, 132, 7, 22], [876, 882, 133, 7, 23], [883, 884, 134, 7, 24]]]}, 'Connective': {'CharacterSpanList': [[796, 800]], 'RawText': 'oder', 'TokenList': [[796, 800, 120, 7, 10]]]}}}

{'ID': 6, 'DocID': '06−08−2020_17:29:47', 'Sense': 'Contingency.Condition. Arg2−as−cond', 'Type': 'Explicit', 'Arg1': {'CharacterSpanList': [[743, 815]], 'RawText': 'So ist etwa unklar , wer Abfindungen erhalten soll , oder was passiert ,', 'TokenList': [[743, 745, 110, 7, 0], [746, 749, 111, 7, 1], [750, 754, 112, 7, 2], [755, 761, 113, 7, 3], [762, 763, 114, 7, 4], [764, 767, 115, 7,

5], [768, 779, 116, 7, 6], [780, 788, 117, 7, 7], [789, 793, 118, 7, 8], [794, 795, 119, 7, 9], [796, 800, 120, 7, 10], [801, 804, 121, 7, 11], [805, 813, 122, 7, 12], [814, 815, 123, 7, 13]]}, 'Arg2': {'CharacterSpanList': [[821, 884]], 'RawText': 'zu wenig Lehrer die Angebote des vorzeitigen Ausstiegs nutzen .', 'TokenList': [[821, 823, 125, 7, 15], [824, 829, 126, 7, 16], [830, 836, 127, 7, 17], [837, 840, 128, 7, 18], [841, 849, 129, 7, 19], [850, 853, 130, 7, 20], [854, 865, 131, 7, 21], [866, 875, 132, 7, 22], [876, 882, 133, 7, 23], [883, 884, 134, 7, 24]]}, 'Connective': {'CharacterSpanList': [[816, 820]], 'RawText': 'wenn', 'TokenList': [[816, 820, 124, 7, 14]]}}

{'ID': 7, 'DocID': '06−08−2020_17:29:47', 'Sense': 'Comparison.Concession. Arg2−as−denier', 'Type': 'Explicit', 'Arg1': {'CharacterSpanList': [[743, 884]], 'RawText': 'So ist etwa unklar , wer Abfindungen erhalten soll , oder was passiert , wenn zu wenig Lehrer die Angebote des vorzeitigen Ausstiegs nutzen .', 'TokenList': [[743, 745, 110, 7, 0], [746, 749, 111, 7, 1], [750, 754, 112, 7, 2], [755, 761, 113, 7, 3], [762, 763, 114, 7, 4], [764, 767, 115, 7, 5], [768, 779, 116, 7, 6], [780, 788, 117, 7, 7], [789, 793, 118, 7, 8], [794, 795, 119, 7, 9], [796, 800, 120, 7, 10], [801, 804, 121, 7, 11], [805, 813, 122, 7, 12], [814, 815, 123, 7, 13], [816, 820, 124, 7, 14], [821, 823, 125, 7, 15], [824, 829, 126, 7, 16], [830, 836, 127, 7, 17], [837, 840, 128, 7, 18], [841, 849, 129, 7, 19], [850, 853, 130, 7, 20], [854, 865, 131, 7, 21], [866, 875, 132, 7, 22], [876, 882, 133, 7, 23], [883, 884, 134, 7, 24]]}, 'Arg2': {'CharacterSpanList': [[893, 957]], 'RawText': 'gibt es zu Reiches Personalpapier eigentlich keine Alternative .', 'TokenList': [[893, 897, 136, 8, 1], [898, 900, 137, 8, 2], [901, 903, 138, 8, 3], [904, 911, 139, 8, 4], [912, 926, 140, 8, 5], [927, 937, 141, 8, 6], [938, 943, 142, 8, 7], [944, 955, 143, 8, 8], [956, 957, 144, 8, 9]]}, 'Connective': {'CharacterSpanList': [[885, 892]], 'RawText': 'Dennoch', 'TokenList': [[885, 892, 135, 8, 0]]}}

{'ID': 8, 'DocID': '06−08−2020_17:29:47', 'Sense': 'Expansion.Conjunction', 'Type': 'Explicit', 'Arg1': {'CharacterSpanList': [[885, 957]], 'RawText': 'Dennoch gibt es zu Reiches Personalpapier eigentlich keine Alternative .', 'TokenList': [[885, 892, 135, 8, 0], [893, 897, 136, 8, 1], [898, 900, 137, 8, 2], [901, 903, 138, 8, 3], [904, 911, 139, 8, 4], [912, 926, 140, 8, 5], [927, 937, 141, 8, 6], [938, 943, 142, 8, 7], [944, 955, 143, 8, 8], [956, 957, 144, 8, 9]]}, 'Arg2': {'CharacterSpanList': [[1024, 1041]], 'RawText': 'die Zeit drängt .', 'TokenList': [[1024, 1027, 158, 10, 1], [1028, 1032, 159, 10, 2], [1033, 1039, 160, 10, 3], [1040, 1041, 161, 10, 4]]}, 'Connective': {'CharacterSpanList': [[1020, 1023]], 'RawText': 'Und', 'TokenList': [[1020, 1023, 157, 10, 0]]}}

{'ID': 9, 'DocID': '06−08−2020_17:29:47', 'Sense': 'Expansion.Disjunction', 'Type': 'Explicit', 'Arg1': {'CharacterSpanList': [[1209, 1230]], 'RawText': 'sparen um jeden Preis', 'TokenList': [[1209, 1215, 188, 13, 1], [1216, 1218, 189, 13, 2], [1219, 1224, 190, 13, 3], [1225, 1230, 191, 13, 4]]}, 'Arg2': {'CharacterSpanList': [[1236, 1263]], 'RawText': 'Priorität für die Bildung .', 'TokenList': [[1236, 1245, 193, 13, 6], [1246, 1249, 194, 13, 7], [1250, 1253, 195, 13, 8], [1254, 1261, 196, 13, 9], [1262, 1263, 197, 13, 10]]}, 'Connective': {'CharacterSpanList': [[1200, 1208], [1231, 1235]], 'RawText': 'Entweder oder', 'TokenList': [[1200, 1208, 187, 13, 0], [1231, 1235, 192, 13, 5]]}}

{'ID': 10, 'DocID': '06−08−2020_17:29:47', 'Sense': 'Comparison.Concession.
Arg2−as−denier', 'Type': 'Implicit', 'Arg1': {'CharacterSpanList': [[0, 62]],
'RawText': 'Auf Eis gelegt \n\nDagmar Ziegler sitzt in der Schuldenfalle .',
'TokenList': [[0, 2, 0, 0, 0], [2, 5, 1, 0, 1], [6, 9, 2, 0, 2], [10, 16, 3, 0, 3], [17,
19, 4, 0, 4], [19, 25, 5, 0, 5], [26, 33, 6, 0, 6], [34, 39, 7, 0, 7], [40, 42, 8, 0,
8], [43, 46, 9, 0, 9], [47, 60, 10, 0, 10], [61, 62, 11, 0, 11]]}, 'Arg2': {'
CharacterSpanList': [[63, 271]], 'RawText': 'Auf Grund der dramatischen
Kassenlage in Brandenburg hat sie jetzt eine seit mehr als einem Jahr
erarbeitete Kabinettsvorlage überraschend auf Eis gelegt und vorgeschlagen
, erst 2003 darüber zu entscheiden .', 'TokenList': [[63, 66, 12, 1, 0], [67,
72, 13, 1, 1], [73, 76, 14, 1, 2], [77, 89, 15, 1, 3], [90, 100, 16, 1, 4], [101,
103, 17, 1, 5], [104, 115, 18, 1, 6], [116, 119, 19, 1, 7], [120, 123, 20, 1, 8],
[124, 129, 21, 1, 9], [130, 134, 22, 1, 10], [135, 139, 23, 1, 11], [140, 144, 24,
1, 12], [145, 148, 25, 1, 13], [149, 154, 26, 1, 14], [155, 159, 27, 1, 15], [160,
171, 28, 1, 16], [172, 188, 29, 1, 17], [189, 201, 30, 1, 18], [202, 205, 31, 1,
19], [206, 209, 32, 1, 20], [210, 216, 33, 1, 21], [217, 220, 34, 1, 22], [221,
234, 35, 1, 23], [235, 236, 36, 1, 24], [237, 241, 37, 1, 25], [242, 246, 38, 1,
26], [247, 254, 39, 1, 27], [255, 257, 40, 1, 28], [258, 269, 41, 1, 29], [270,
271, 42, 1, 30]]}, 'Connective': {'CharacterSpanList': [], 'RawText': '', '
TokenList': []}}
{'ID': 11, 'DocID': '06−08−2020_17:29:47', 'Sense': 'Comparison.Concession.
Arg2−as−denier', 'Type': 'Implicit', 'Arg1': {'CharacterSpanList': [[63,
271]], 'RawText': 'Auf Grund der dramatischen Kassenlage in Brandenburg
hat sie jetzt eine seit mehr als einem Jahr erarbeitete Kabinettsvorlage ü
berraschend auf Eis gelegt und vorgeschlagen , erst 2003 darüber zu
entscheiden .', 'TokenList': [[63, 66, 12, 1, 0], [67, 72, 13, 1, 1], [73, 76, 14,
1, 2], [77, 89, 15, 1, 3], [90, 100, 16, 1, 4], [101, 103, 17, 1, 5], [104, 115, 18,
1, 6], [116, 119, 19, 1, 7], [120, 123, 20, 1, 8], [124, 129, 21, 1, 9], [130, 134,
22, 1, 10], [135, 139, 23, 1, 11], [140, 144, 24, 1, 12], [145, 148, 25, 1, 13],
[149, 154, 26, 1, 14], [155, 159, 27, 1, 15], [160, 171, 28, 1, 16], [172, 188, 29,
1, 17], [189, 201, 30, 1, 18], [202, 205, 31, 1, 19], [206, 209, 32, 1, 20], [210,
216, 33, 1, 21], [217, 220, 34, 1, 22], [221, 234, 35, 1, 23], [235, 236, 36, 1,
24], [237, 241, 37, 1, 25], [242, 246, 38, 1, 26], [247, 254, 39, 1, 27], [255,
257, 40, 1, 28], [258, 269, 41, 1, 29], [270, 271, 42, 1, 30]]}, 'Arg2': {'
CharacterSpanList': [[272, 383]], 'RawText': 'Überraschend , weil das
Finanz− und das Bildungsressort das Lehrerpersonalkonzept gemeinsam
entwickelt hatten .', 'TokenList': [[272, 284, 43, 2, 0], [285, 286, 44, 2, 1],
[287, 291, 45, 2, 2], [292, 295, 46, 2, 3], [296, 303, 47, 2, 4], [304, 307, 48, 2,
5], [308, 311, 49, 2, 6], [312, 327, 50, 2, 7], [328, 331, 51, 2, 8], [332, 353, 52,
2, 9], [354, 363, 53, 2, 10], [364, 374, 54, 2, 11], [375, 381, 55, 2, 12], [382,
383, 56, 2, 13]]}, 'Connective': {'CharacterSpanList': [], 'RawText': '', '
TokenList': []}}
{'ID': 12, 'DocID': '06−08−2020_17:29:47', 'Sense': 'Contingency.Cause.Reason
', 'Type': 'Implicit', 'Arg1': {'CharacterSpanList': [[384, 443]], 'RawText': '
Der Rückzieher der Finanzministerin ist aber verständlich .', 'TokenList':
[[384, 387, 57, 3, 0], [388, 398, 58, 3, 1], [399, 402, 59, 3, 2], [403, 419, 60, 3,
3], [420, 423, 61, 3, 4], [424, 428, 62, 3, 5], [429, 441, 63, 3, 6], [442, 443,

64, 3, 7]]}, 'Arg2': {'CharacterSpanList': [[444, 594]], 'RawText': 'Es dürfte derzeit schwer zu vermitteln sein , weshalb ein Ressort pauschal von kü nftigen Einsparungen ausgenommen werden soll auf Kosten der anderen .', 'TokenList': [[444, 446, 65, 4, 0], [447, 453, 66, 4, 1], [454, 461, 67, 4, 2], [462, 468, 68, 4, 3], [469, 471, 69, 4, 4], [472, 482, 70, 4, 5], [483, 487, 71, 4, 6], [488, 489, 72, 4, 7], [490, 497, 73, 4, 8], [498, 501, 74, 4, 9], [502, 509, 75, 4, 10], [510, 518, 76, 4, 11], [519, 522, 77, 4, 12], [523, 532, 78, 4, 13], [533, 545, 79, 4, 14], [546, 557, 80, 4, 15], [558, 564, 81, 4, 16], [565, 569, 82, 4, 17], [570, 573, 83, 4, 18], [574, 580, 84, 4, 19], [581, 584, 85, 4, 20], [585, 592, 86, 4, 21], [593, 594, 87, 4, 22]]}, 'Connective': {'CharacterSpanList': [], 'RawText': '', 'TokenList': []}}

{'ID': 13, 'DocID': '06−08−2020_17:29:47', 'Sense': 'Expansion.Level−of−detail.Arg2−as−detail', 'Type': 'Implicit', 'Arg1': {'CharacterSpanList': [[444, 594]], 'RawText': 'Es dürfte derzeit schwer zu vermitteln sein , weshalb ein Ressort pauschal von künftigen Einsparungen ausgenommen werden soll auf Kosten der anderen .', 'TokenList': [[444, 446, 65, 4, 0], [447, 453, 66, 4, 1], [454, 461, 67, 4, 2], [462, 468, 68, 4, 3], [469, 471, 69, 4, 4], [472, 482, 70, 4, 5], [483, 487, 71, 4, 6], [488, 489, 72, 4, 7], [490, 497, 73, 4, 8], [498, 501, 74, 4, 9], [502, 509, 75, 4, 10], [510, 518, 76, 4, 11], [519, 522, 77, 4, 12], [523, 532, 78, 4, 13], [533, 545, 79, 4, 14], [546, 557, 80, 4, 15], [558, 564, 81, 4, 16], [565, 569, 82, 4, 17], [570, 573, 83, 4, 18], [574, 580, 84, 4, 19], [581, 584, 85, 4, 20], [585, 592, 86, 4, 21], [593, 594, 87, 4, 22]]}, 'Arg2': {'CharacterSpanList': [[595, 693]], 'RawText': 'Reiches Ministerkollegen werden mit Argusaugen darüber wachen , dass das Konzept wasserdicht ist .', 'TokenList': [[595, 602, 88, 5, 0], [603, 619, 89, 5, 1], [620, 626, 90, 5, 2], [627, 630, 91, 5, 3], [631, 641, 92, 5, 4], [642, 649, 93, 5, 5], [650, 656, 94, 5, 6], [657, 658, 95, 5, 7], [659, 663, 96, 5, 8], [664, 667, 97, 5, 9], [668, 675, 98, 5, 10], [676, 687, 99, 5, 11], [688, 691, 100, 5, 12], [692, 693, 101, 5, 13]]}, 'Connective': {'CharacterSpanList': [], 'RawText': '', 'TokenList': []}}

{'ID': 14, 'DocID': '06−08−2020_17:29:47', 'Sense': 'Contingency.Cause.Result', 'Type': 'Implicit', 'Arg1': {'CharacterSpanList': [[595, 693]], 'RawText': 'Reiches Ministerkollegen werden mit Argusaugen darüber wachen , dass das Konzept wasserdicht ist .', 'TokenList': [[595, 602, 88, 5, 0], [603, 619, 89, 5, 1], [620, 626, 90, 5, 2], [627, 630, 91, 5, 3], [631, 641, 92, 5, 4], [642, 649, 93, 5, 5], [650, 656, 94, 5, 6], [657, 658, 95, 5, 7], [659, 663, 96, 5, 8], [664, 667, 97, 5, 9], [668, 675, 98, 5, 10], [676, 687, 99, 5, 11], [688, 691, 100, 5, 12], [692, 693, 101, 5, 13]]}, 'Arg2': {'CharacterSpanList': [[694, 742]], 'RawText': 'Tatsächlich gibt es noch etliche offene Fragen .', 'TokenList': [[694, 705, 102, 6, 0], [706, 710, 103, 6, 1], [711, 713, 104, 6, 2], [714, 718, 105, 6, 3], [719, 726, 106, 6, 4], [727, 733, 107, 6, 5], [734, 740, 108, 6, 6], [741, 742, 109, 6, 7]]}, 'Connective': {'CharacterSpanList': [], 'RawText': '', 'TokenList': []}}

{'ID': 15, 'DocID': '06−08−2020_17:29:47', 'Sense': 'Contingency.Cause.Reason', 'Type': 'Implicit', 'Arg1': {'CharacterSpanList': [[694, 742]], 'RawText': 'Tatsächlich gibt es noch etliche offene Fragen .', 'TokenList': [[694, 705, 102, 6, 0], [706, 710, 103, 6, 1], [711, 713, 104, 6, 2], [714, 718, 105, 6, 3],

[719, 726, 106, 6, 4], [727, 733, 107, 6, 5], [734, 740, 108, 6, 6], [741, 742, 109, 6, 7]]}, 'Arg2': {'CharacterSpanList': [[743, 884]], 'RawText': 'So ist etwa unklar , wer Abfindungen erhalten soll , oder was passiert , wenn zu wenig Lehrer die Angebote des vorzeitigen Ausstiegs nutzen .', 'TokenList': [[743, 745, 110, 7, 0], [746, 749, 111, 7, 1], [750, 754, 112, 7, 2], [755, 761, 113, 7, 3], [762, 763, 114, 7, 4], [764, 767, 115, 7, 5], [768, 779, 116, 7, 6], [780, 788, 117, 7, 7], [789, 793, 118, 7, 8], [794, 795, 119, 7, 9], [796, 800, 120, 7, 10], [801, 804, 121, 7, 11], [805, 813, 122, 7, 12], [814, 815, 123, 7, 13], [816, 820, 124, 7, 14], [821, 823, 125, 7, 15], [824, 829, 126, 7, 16], [830, 836, 127, 7, 17], [837, 840, 128, 7, 18], [841, 849, 129, 7, 19], [850, 853, 130, 7, 20], [854, 865, 131, 7, 21], [866, 875, 132, 7, 22], [876, 882, 133, 7, 23], [883, 884, 134, 7, 24]]}, 'Connective': {'CharacterSpanList': [], 'RawText': '', 'TokenList': []}}

{'ID': 16, 'DocID': '06−08−2020_17:29:47', 'Sense': 'Contingency.Cause.Reason', 'Type': 'Implicit', 'Arg1': {'CharacterSpanList': [[885, 957]], 'RawText': ' Dennoch gibt es zu Reiches Personalpapier eigentlich keine Alternative .', ' TokenList': [[885, 892, 135, 8, 0], [893, 897, 136, 8, 1], [898, 900, 137, 8, 2], [901, 903, 138, 8, 3], [904, 911, 139, 8, 4], [912, 926, 140, 8, 5], [927, 937, 141, 8, 6], [938, 943, 142, 8, 7], [944, 955, 143, 8, 8], [956, 957, 144, 8, 9]]}, ' Arg2': {'CharacterSpanList': [[958, 1019]], 'RawText': 'Das Land hat kü nftig zu wenig Arbeit für zu viele Pädagogen .', 'TokenList': [[958, 961, 145, 9, 0], [962, 966, 146, 9, 1], [967, 970, 147, 9, 2], [971, 978, 148, 9, 3], [979, 981, 149, 9, 4], [982, 987, 150, 9, 5], [988, 994, 151, 9, 6], [995, 998, 152, 9, 7], [999, 1001, 153, 9, 8], [1002, 1007, 154, 9, 9], [1008, 1017, 155, 9, 10], [1018, 1019, 156, 9, 11]]}, 'Connective': {'CharacterSpanList': [], 'RawText': '', 'TokenList': []}}

{'ID': 17, 'DocID': '06−08−2020_17:29:47', 'Sense': 'Expansion.Level−of− detail.Arg2−as−detail', 'Type': 'Implicit', 'Arg1': {'CharacterSpanList': [[958, 1019]], 'RawText': 'Das Land hat künftig zu wenig Arbeit für zu viele Pädagogen .', 'TokenList': [[958, 961, 145, 9, 0], [962, 966, 146, 9, 1], [967, 970, 147, 9, 2], [971, 978, 148, 9, 3], [979, 981, 149, 9, 4], [982, 987, 150, 9, 5], [988, 994, 151, 9, 6], [995, 998, 152, 9, 7], [999, 1001, 153, 9, 8], [1002, 1007, 154, 9, 9], [1008, 1017, 155, 9, 10], [1018, 1019, 156, 9, 11]]}, 'Arg2': {'CharacterSpanList': [[1020, 1041]], 'RawText': 'Und die Zeit drängt .', ' TokenList': [[1020, 1023, 157, 10, 0], [1024, 1027, 158, 10, 1], [1028, 1032, 159, 10, 2], [1033, 1039, 160, 10, 3], [1040, 1041, 161, 10, 4]]}, 'Connective': {'CharacterSpanList': [], 'RawText': '', 'TokenList': []}}

{'ID': 18, 'DocID': '06−08−2020_17:29:47', 'Sense': 'Contingency.Cause.Reason', 'Type': 'Implicit', 'Arg1': {'CharacterSpanList': [[1020, 1041]], 'RawText': 'Und die Zeit drängt .', 'TokenList': [[1020, 1023, 157, 10, 0], [1024, 1027, 158, 10, 1], [1028, 1032, 159, 10, 2], [1033, 1039, 160, 10, 3], [1040, 1041, 161, 10, 4]]}, 'Arg2': {'CharacterSpanList': [[1042, 1142]], 'RawText': 'Der große Einbruch der Schülerzahlen an den weiterführenden Schulen beginnt bereits im Herbst 2003 .', 'TokenList': [[1042, 1045, 162, 11, 0], [1046, 1051, 163, 11, 1], [1052, 1060, 164, 11, 2], [1061, 1064, 165, 11, 3], [1065, 1078, 166, 11, 4], [1079, 1081, 167, 11, 5], [1082, 1085, 168, 11, 6], [1086, 1101, 169, 11, 7], [1102, 1109, 170, 11, 8], [1110, 1117, 171, 11, 9], [1118, 1125,

140

172, 11, 10], [1126, 1128, 173, 11, 11], [1129, 1135, 174, 11, 12], [1136, 1140, 175, 11, 13], [1141, 1142, 176, 11, 14]]]}, 'Connective': {'CharacterSpanList': [], 'RawText': '', 'TokenList': []}}
{'ID': 19, 'DocID': '06−08−2020_17:29:47', 'Sense': 'Contingency.Cause.Result', 'Type': 'Implicit', 'Arg1': {'CharacterSpanList': [[1042, 1142]], 'RawText': 'Der große Einbruch der Schülerzahlen an den weiterführenden Schulen beginnt bereits im Herbst 2003 .', 'TokenList': [[1042, 1045, 162, 11, 0], [1046, 1051, 163, 11, 1], [1052, 1060, 164, 11, 2], [1061, 1064, 165, 11, 3], [1065, 1078, 166, 11, 4], [1079, 1081, 167, 11, 5], [1082, 1085, 168, 11, 6], [1086, 1101, 169, 11, 7], [1102, 1109, 170, 11, 8], [1110, 1117, 171, 11, 9], [1118, 1125, 172, 11, 10], [1126, 1128, 173, 11, 11], [1129, 1135, 174, 11, 12], [1136, 1140, 175, 11, 13], [1141, 1142, 176, 11, 14]]]}, 'Arg2': {'CharacterSpanList': [[1143, 1199]], 'RawText': 'Die Regierung muss sich entscheiden , und zwar schnell .', 'TokenList': [[1143, 1146, 177, 12, 0], [1147, 1156, 178, 12, 1], [1157, 1161, 179, 12, 2], [1162, 1166, 180, 12, 3], [1167, 1178, 181, 12, 4], [1179, 1180, 182, 12, 5], [1181, 1184, 183, 12, 6], [1185, 1189, 184, 12, 7], [1190, 1197, 185, 12, 8], [1198, 1199, 186, 12, 9]]]}, 'Connective': {'CharacterSpanList': [], 'RawText': '', 'TokenList': []}}
{'ID': 20, 'DocID': '06−08−2020_17:29:47', 'Sense': 'Contingency.Cause.Reason', 'Type': 'Implicit', 'Arg1': {'CharacterSpanList': [[1143, 1199]], 'RawText': 'Die Regierung muss sich entscheiden , und zwar schnell .', 'TokenList': [[1143, 1146, 177, 12, 0], [1147, 1156, 178, 12, 1], [1157, 1161, 179, 12, 2], [1162, 1166, 180, 12, 3], [1167, 1178, 181, 12, 4], [1179, 1180, 182, 12, 5], [1181, 1184, 183, 12, 6], [1185, 1189, 184, 12, 7], [1190, 1197, 185, 12, 8], [1198, 1199, 186, 12, 9]]]}, 'Arg2': {'CharacterSpanList': [[1200, 1263]], 'RawText': 'Entweder sparen um jeden Preis oder Priorität für die Bildung .', 'TokenList': [[1200, 1208, 187, 13, 0], [1209, 1215, 188, 13, 1], [1216, 1218, 189, 13, 2], [1219, 1224, 190, 13, 3], [1225, 1230, 191, 13, 4], [1231, 1235, 192, 13, 5], [1236, 1245, 193, 13, 6], [1246, 1249, 194, 13, 7], [1250, 1253, 195, 13, 8], [1254, 1261, 196, 13, 9], [1262, 1263, 197, 13, 10]]]}, 'Connective': {'CharacterSpanList': [], 'RawText': '', 'TokenList': []}}
{'ID': 21, 'DocID': '06−08−2020_17:29:47', 'Sense': 'Expansion.Conjunction', 'Type': 'Implicit', 'Arg1': {'CharacterSpanList': [[1200, 1263]], 'RawText': 'Entweder sparen um jeden Preis oder Priorität für die Bildung .', 'TokenList': [[1200, 1208, 187, 13, 0], [1209, 1215, 188, 13, 1], [1216, 1218, 189, 13, 2], [1219, 1224, 190, 13, 3], [1225, 1230, 191, 13, 4], [1231, 1235, 192, 13, 5], [1236, 1245, 193, 13, 6], [1246, 1249, 194, 13, 7], [1250, 1253, 195, 13, 8], [1254, 1261, 196, 13, 9], [1262, 1263, 197, 13, 10]]]}, 'Arg2': {'CharacterSpanList': [[1264, 1265]], 'RawText': '', 'TokenList': [[1264, 1265, 198, 14, 0]]}, 'Connective': {'CharacterSpanList': [], 'RawText': '', 'TokenList': []}}
]

Appendix C

Parser Documentation

C.1. Parser: Installation & Usage

There are two ways to get this parser up and running. The easy way is by building and running the docker version. The slightly more elaborate way is by downloading and installing all requirements yourself. Both are described below.

C.1.1. Docker (easy)

- Clone the repository:
  ```
  git clone \
  https://github.com/PeterBourgonje/GermanShallow
  DiscourseParser
  ```

- cd into the cloned folder, then build the Docker container:
  ```
  docker build -t gsdp .
  ```
  where gsdp is the container name, i.e. can be anything you want, as long as it matches this when running the container.

- After a successful build, start the container:
  ```
  docker run -p5500:5000 -it gsdp
  ```
  Running the container starts the bert-serving server that is required, and starts the Flask app that exposes the two endpoints; one for training and one for parsing. This (esp. the bert-serving server) takes a few seconds to start. Wait for the message:
  ```
  all set, ready to serve request!
  ```
  to show up in your terminal.

- Before you can start parsing, you need to train the parser. This is best done with curl. As per the command above, the flask app is exposed through the docker container at port 5500, with this the command to train the parser is:
  ```
  curl localhost:5500/train
  ```
  This takes a few minutes (2 minutes on a laptop/CPU with 2.2GhZ and 24GB RAM), wait for the response message:
  ```
  INFO: Successfully trained models
  ```

- The parser is now trained and ready to go. The following curl command parses the input file located at <path/to/local/file.txt>:
  ```
  curl -X POST -F input=@<path/to/local/file.txt>
  localhost:5500/parse
  ```

Parsing is not particularly fast (ca. 6.5 tokens per second on a laptop/CPU with 2.2GhZ and 24GB RAM), so please be patient.

C.1.2. Manual (less easy)

Should the Docker version not work for some reason, here is how to get it up and running manually:

- Clone the repository:
  ```
  git clone \
  https://github.com/PeterBourgonje/GermanShallow
  DiscourseParser
  ```

- Download the Stanford Parser:
  ```
  wget \
  https://nlp.stanford.edu/software/stanford-parser-
  full-2018-10-17.zip
  ```
  and unzip it to a local folder on your system.

- Download the German Bert model:
  ```
  wget \
  https://int-deepset-models-bert.s3.eu-central-1.
  amazonaws.com
  /tensorflow/bert-base-german-cased.zip
  ```
  and unzip it to a local folder on your system.

- Clone the DiMLex repository to your local system:
  ```
  git clone https://github.com/discourse-lab/dimlex
  ```

- Clone the PCC repository to your local system:
  `git clone https://github.com/PeterBourgonje/pcc2.2`

- Install all required python packages:
  `pip install -r requirements.txt`

- Modify the paths in `config.ini` to match your system configuration. The variables you have to modify are `pccdir`, `dimlexdir`, `parserdir` and `modeldir`. Make sure these point to the locations where you have just downloaded/unzipped/cloned the respective modules.

- Manually start a bert-serving server:
  `bert-serving-start -model_dir <location/to/bert/ model> \`
  `-num_worker=4 -max_seq_len=52`, where `<location/to/ bert/model>` points to where you just unzipped the Bert model. You can use a higher `max_seq_len` value if you wish (this merely controls the number of tokens after which input to vector representation is cut off). Wait for the message `all set, ready to serve request!` to show up in your terminal.

- Start the flask app:
  `python3 Parser.py`
  You can specify a port number (optionally) with the `-port` flag (followed by a white space, then the desired port number; by default 5000 is taken).

- Before you can start parsing, you need to train the parser. This is best done with curl:
  `curl localhost:5000/train`
  This takes a few minutes (2 minutes on a laptop/CPU with 2.2GhZ and 24GB RAM), wait for the response message:
  `INFO: Successfully trained models`

- The parser is now trained and ready to go. The following curl command parses the input file located at
  `<path/to/local/file.txt>`:`curl -X POST -F input=@<path /to/local/file.txt> localhost:5000/parse`

Bibliography

Aesop Rock (2005). *The Living Human Curiosity Sideshow*. Definitve Jux Records, New York City.

Afantenos, S., Asher, N., Benamara, F., Bras, M., Fabre, C., Hodac, M., Draoulec, A. L., Muller, P., Péry-Woodley, M.-P., Prévot, L., Rebeyrolles, J., Tanguy, L., Vergez-Couret, M., and Vieu, L. (2012). An empirical resource for discovering cognitive principles of discourse organisation: the ANNODIS corpus. In *Proceedings of the Eighth International Conference on Language Resources and Evaluation (LREC'12)*, pages 2727–2734, Istanbul, Turkey. European Language Resources Association (ELRA).

Alemany, L. A. i. (2005). *Representing discourse for automatic text summarization via shallow NLP techniques*. PhD dissertation, Universitat de Barcelona.

Asher, N. (1993). *Reference to Abstract Objects in Discourse*. SLAP 50, Dordrecht, Kluwer.

Asher, N., Hunter, J., Morey, M., Farah, B., and Afantenos, S. (2016). Discourse structure and dialogue acts in multiparty dialogue: the STAC corpus. In *Proceedings of the Tenth International Conference on Language Resources and Evaluation (LREC'16)*, pages 2721–2727, Portorož, Slovenia. European Language Resources Association (ELRA).

Asher, N., Lascarides, A., Bird, S., Boguraev, B., Hindle, D., Kay, M., McDonald, D., and Uszkoreit, H. (2003). *Logics of Conversation*. Studies in Natural Language Processing. Cambridge University Press.

Bai, H. and Zhao, H. (2018). Deep enhanced representation for implicit discourse relation recognition. In *Proceedings of the 27th International Conference on Computational Linguistics*, pages 571–

583, Santa Fe, New Mexico, USA. Association for Computational Linguistics.

Baldridge, J. and Elwell, R. (2008). Discourse connective argument identification with connective specific rankers. In *2008 IEEE International Conference on Semantic Computing(ICSC)*, pages 198–205.

Biran, O. and McKeown, K. (2015). PDTB discourse parsing as a tagging task: The two taggers approach. In *Proceedings of the 16th Annual Meeting of the Special Interest Group on Discourse and Dialogue*, pages 96–104, Prague, Czech Republic. Association for Computational Linguistics.

Biran, O. and Rambow, O. (2011). Identifying justifications in written dialogs by classifying text as argumentative. *International Journal of Semantic Computing*, 5(4):363–381.

Bird, S. and Loper, E. (2004). NLTK: The natural language toolkit. In *Proceedings of the ACL Interactive Poster and Demonstration Sessions*, pages 214–217, Barcelona, Spain. Association for Computational Linguistics.

Bourgonje, P., Grishina, Y., and Stede, M. (2017). Toward a bilingual lexical database on connectives: Exploiting a German/Italian parallel corpus. In *Proceedings of the Fourth Italian Conference on Computational Linguistics*, Rome, Italy.

Bourgonje, P., Hoek, J., Evers-Vermeul, J., Redeker, G., Sanders, T., and Stede, M. (2018). Constructing a Lexicon of Dutch Discourse Connectives. *Computational Linguistics in the Netherlands Journal*, 8:163–175.

Bourgonje, P. and Schäfer, R. (2019). Multi-lingual and cross-genre discourse unit segmentation. In *Proceedings of the Workshop on Discourse Relation Parsing and Treebanking 2019*, pages 105–114, Minneapolis, MN. Association for Computational Linguistics.

Bourgonje, P. and Stede, M. (2018a). Identifying explicit discourse connectives in German. In *Proceedings of the 19th Annual SIGdial Meeting on Discourse and Dialogue*, pages 327–331, Melbourne, Australia. Association for Computational Linguistics.

Bourgonje, P. and Stede, M. (2018b). The Potsdam Commentary Corpus 2.1 in ANNIS3. In *Proceedings of the 17th International Workshop on Treebanks and Linguistic Theory*, pages 31–38, Oslo, Norway. Linköping University Electronic Press, Linköpings universitet.

Bourgonje, P. and Stede, M. (2019). Explicit Discourse Argument Extraction for German. In *Proceedings of the 21st International Conference on Text, Speech and Dialogue*, pages 32–44, Ljubljana, Slovenia.

Bourgonje, P. and Stede, M. (2020a). Exploiting a lexical resource for discourse connective disambiguation in German. In *Proceedings of the 28th International Conference on Computational Linguistics*, pages 5737–5748, Barcelona, Spain (Online).

Bourgonje, P. and Stede, M. (2020b). The Potsdam commentary corpus 2.2: Extending annotations for shallow discourse parsing. In *Proceedings of The 12th Language Resources and Evaluation Conference (LREC'20)*, pages 1061–1066, Marseille, France. European Language Resources Association (ELRA).

Bourgonje, P. and Zolotarenko, O. (2019). Toward cross-theory discourse relation annotation. In *Proceedings of the Workshop on Discourse Relation Parsing and Treebanking 2019*, pages 7–11, Minneapolis, MN. Association for Computational Linguistics.

Brants, S., Dipper, S., Eisenberg, P., Hansen-Schirra, S., König, E., Lezius, W., Rohrer, C., Smith, G., and Uszkoreit, H. (2004). TIGER: Linguistic Interpretation of a German Corpus. *Research on Language and Computation*, 2(4):597–620.

Brants, S., Dipper, S., Hansen, S., Lezius, W., and Smith, G. (2002). The TIGER treebank. In *Proceedings of the workshop on treebanks and linguistic theories*, pages 24–41.

Briz, A., Bordería, S. P., and Portolés, J. (2008). Diccionario de partículas discursivas del español.

Burstein, J., Kukich, K., Wolff, S., Lu, C., and Chodorow, M. (1998). Enriching automated essay scoring using discourse marking. In *Discourse Relations and Discourse Markers*, pages 15–21.

Cao, S., da Cunha, I., and Iruskieta, M. (2018). The RST Spanish-Chinese treebank. In *Proceedings of the Joint Workshop on Linguistic Annotation, Multiword Expressions and Constructions (LAW-MWE-CxG-2018)*, pages 156–166, Santa Fe, New Mexico, USA. Association for Computational Linguistics.

Cardoso, P., Maziero, E., Jorge, M., Seno, E., Di Felippo, A., Rino, L., Nunes, M., and Pardo, T. (2011). CSTNews - A Discourse-Annotated Corpus for Single and Multi-Document Summarization of News Texts in Brazilian Portuguese. In *Proceedings of the 3rd RST Brazilian Meeting*, pages 88–105. Cuiabá/MT, Brazil.

Carlson, L., Marcu, D., and Okurowski, M. E. (2002). RST Discourse Treebank, LDC2002T07.

Cartoni, B., Zufferey, S., and Meyer, T. (2013). Annotating the meaning of discourse connectives by looking at their translation: The translation-spotting technique. *Dialogue & Discourse*, 4(2):65–86.

Church, K. (2011). A pendulum swung too far. *Linguistic Issues in Language Technology*, 6(5):1–27.

Cohen, R. (1984). A computational theory of the function of clue words in argument understanding. In *10th International Conference on Computational Linguistics and 22nd Annual Meeting of the Association for Computational Linguistics*, pages 251–258, Stanford, California, USA. Association for Computational Linguistics.

da Cunha, I., Torres-Moreno, J.-M., and Sierra, G. (2011). On the Development of the RST Spanish Treebank. In *Proceedings of the 5th Linguistic Annotation Workshop*, pages 1–10, Stroudsburg, PA, USA. Association for Computational Linguistics.

Dai, Z. and Huang, R. (2018). Improving implicit discourse relation classification by modeling inter-dependencies of discourse units in a paragraph. In *Proceedings of the 2018 Conference of the North American Chapter of the Association for Computational Linguistics: Human Language Technologies, Volume 1 (Long Papers)*, pages 141–151, New Orleans, Louisiana. Association for Computational Linguistics.

Dale, R. (1991). The role of punctuation in discourse structure. In *Proceedings of AAAI Fall Symposium on Discourse Structure in Natural Language Understanding and Generation*, pages 13–14, Asilomar, CA.

Danlos, L., Rysova, K., Rysova, M., and Stede, M. (2018). Primary and secondary discourse connectives: definitions and lexicons. *Dialogue and Discourse*, 9(1):50–78.

Das, D. (2014). *Signalling of Coherence Relations in Discourse*. PhD thesis, Simon Fraser University.

Das, D., Scheffler, T., Bourgonje, P., and Stede, M. (2018). Constructing a lexicon of English discourse connectives. In *Proceedings of the 19th Annual SIGdial Meeting on Discourse and Dialogue*, pages 360–365, Melbourne, Australia. Association for Computational Linguistics.

Das, D., Stede, M., Ghosh, S. S., and Chatterjee, L. (2020). DiMLex-bangla: A lexicon of bangla discourse connectives. In *Proceedings of the 12th International Conference on Language Resources and Evaluation (LREC'20)*, pages 1097–1102, Marseille, France. European Language Resources Association (ELRA).

Das, D. and Taboada, M. (2018). RST Signalling Corpus: a corpus of signals of coherence relations. *Language Resources and Evaluation*, 52(1):149–184.

Devlin, J., Chang, M.-W., Lee, K., and Toutanova, K. (2019). BERT: Pre-training of deep bidirectional transformers for language understanding. In *Proceedings of the 2019 Conference of the North American Chapter of the Association for Computational Linguistics: Human Language Technologies, Volume 1 (Long and Short Papers)*, pages 4171–4186, Minneapolis, Minnesota. Association for Computational Linguistics.

Dines, N., Lee, A., Miltsakaki, E., Prasad, R., Joshi, A., and Webber, B. (2005). Attribution and the (non-)alignment of syntactic and discourse arguments of connectives. In *Proceedings of the Workshop on Frontiers in Corpus Annotations II: Pie in the Sky*, CorpusAnno '05, page 29–36, USA. Association for Computational Linguistics.

Dipper, S. and Stede, M. (2006). Disambiguating potential connectives. In *Proceedings of the KONVENS Conference*, Konstanz.

Evers-Vermeul, J., Hoek, J., and Scholman, M. (2017). On temporality in discourse annotation: Theoretical and practical considerations. *Dialogue & Discourse*, 8(2):1–20.

Feltracco, A., Jezek, E., Magnini, B., and Stede, M. (2016). Lico: A lexicon of Italian connectives. In *Proceedings of the 3rd Italian Conference on Computational Linguistics (CLiC-it)*, pages 141–145, Napoli, Italy.

Feng, V. W. and Hirst, G. (2014). A linear-time bottom-up discourse parser with constraints and post-editing. In *Proceedings of the 52nd Annual Meeting of the Association for Computational Linguistics (Volume 1: Long Papers)*, pages 511–521, Baltimore, Maryland. Association for Computational Linguistics.

Ferrari, A. (2010). *Connettivi*. Istituto della Enciclopedia Italiana.

Fielding, R. T. (2000). *Architectural Styles and the Design of Network-Based Software Architectures*. PhD thesis, University of California, Irvine.

Gao, Q. and Vogel, S. (2008). Parallel implementations of word alignment tool. In *Software Engineering, Testing, and Quality Assurance for Natural Language Processing*, SETQA-NLP '08, pages 49–

57, Columbus, Ohio. Association for Computational Linguistics.

Grave, E., Bojanowski, P., Gupta, P., Joulin, A., and Mikolov, T. (2018). Learning word vectors for 157 languages. In *Proceedings of the 11th International Conference on Language Resources and Evaluation (LREC'18)*, pages 3483–3487.

Grosz, B. J. and Sidner, C. L. (1986). Attention, intentions, and the structure of discourse. *Computational Linguistics*, 12(3):175–204.

Heilman, M. and Sagae, K. (2015). Fast rhetorical structure theory discourse parsing. *CoRR*, abs/1505.02425.

Hernault, H., Prendinger, H., duVerle, D. A., and Ishizuka, M. (2010). HILDA: A Discourse Parser Using Support Vector Machine Classification. *Dialogue & Discourse*, 1(3):1–33.

Hewett, F., Prakash Rane, R., Harlacher, N., and Stede, M. (2019). The utility of discourse parsing features for predicting argumentation structure. In *Proceedings of the 6th Workshop on Argument Mining*, pages 98–103, Florence, Italy. Association for Computational Linguistics.

Hoek, J. (2018). *Making sense of discourse: On discourse segmentation and the linguistic marking of coherence relations*. PhD thesis, Utrecht University.

Hooda, S. and Kosseim, L. (2017). Argument labeling of explicit discourse relations using LSTM neural networks. In Mitkov, R. and Angelova, G., editors, *Proceedings of the International Conference Recent Advances in Natural Language Processing, RANLP 2017, Varna, Bulgaria, September 2 - 8, 2017*, pages 309–315. INCOMA Ltd.

Hovy, E. and Maier, E. (1993). Parsimonious or profligate: How many and which discourse structure relations? Technical Report ISI/RR-93-373, Information Sciences Institute.

Iruskieta, M., Aranzabe, M., de Ilarraza, A. D., Gonzalez, I., Lersundi, I., and de Lacalle, O. L. (2013). The RST Basque TreeBank: an online search interface to check rhetorical relations. In *4th. Workshop RST and Discourse Studies*, pages 40–49. Sociedad Brasileira de Computacao, Fortaleza, CE, Brasil.

Jacobs, J. (2001). The dimensions of topic-comment. *Linguistics*, 39:641–682.

Ji, Y. and Eisenstein, J. (2014). Representation learning for text-level discourse parsing. In *Proceedings of the 52nd Annual Meeting of the Association for Computational Linguistics (Volume 1: Long*

Papers), pages 13–24, Baltimore, Maryland. Association for Computational Linguistics.

Ji, Y. and Eisenstein, J. (2015). One vector is not enough: Entity-augmented distributed semantics for discourse relations. *Transactions of the Association for Computational Linguistics*, 3:329–344.

Joty, S., Carenini, G., and Ng, R. T. (2015). CODRA: A novel discriminative framework for rhetorical analysis. *Computational Linguistics*, 41(3):385–435.

Kamp, H. and Reyle, U. (1993). *From Discourse to Logic - Introduction to Modeltheoretic Semantics of Natural Language, Formal Logic and Discourse Representation Theory*, volume 42 of *Studies in linguistics and philosophy*. Springer.

Keskes, I., Benamara, F., and Belguith, L. H. (2014). Learning explicit and implicit arabic discourse relations. *Journal of King Saud University*, 26(4):398–416.

Kirschner, C., Eckle-Kohler, J., and Gurevych, I. (2015). Linking the thoughts: Analysis of argumentation structures in scientific publications. In *Proceedings of the 2nd Workshop on Argumentation Mining*, pages 1–11, Denver, CO. Association for Computational Linguistics.

Knott, A. (1996). *A data-driven methodology for motivating a set of coherence relations*. PhD thesis, University of Edinburgh, UK.

Knott, A. and Dale, R. (1994). Using linguistic phenomena to motivate a set of coherence relations. *Discourse Processes*, 18:35–62.

Koehn, P. (2005). Europarl: A Parallel Corpus for Statistical Machine Translation. In *Conference Proceedings: the 10th Machine Translation Summit*, pages 79–86, Phuket, Thailand. AAMT, AAMT.

Kong, F., Li, S., Li, J., Zhu, M., and Zhou, G. (2016). SoNLP-DP system for ConLL-2016 English shallow discourse parsing. In *Proceedings of the 20th Conference on Computational Natural Language Learning: Shared Task (CoNLL Shared Task 2016)*, pages 65–69, Berlin, Germany. Association for Computational Linguistics.

Krause, T. and Zeldes, A. (2016). ANNIS3: A new architecture for generic corpus query and visualization. *Digital Scholarship in the Humanities*, 31(1):118–139.

Laali, M., Cianflone, A., and Kosseim, L. (2016). The CLaC discourse parser at CoNLL-2016. In *Proceedings of the 20th Conference on Computational Natural Language Learning: Shared Task (CoNLL Shared Task 2016)*, pages 92–99, Berlin, Germany. Association for

Computational Linguistics.

Laali, M. and Kosseim, L. (2014). Inducing Discourse Connectives from Parallel Texts. In *Proceedings of COLING 2014, the 25th International Conference on Computational Linguistics: Technical Papers*, pages 610–619, Dublin, Ireland. Dublin City University and Association for Computational Linguistics.

Lapata, M. and Lascarides, A. (2004). Inferring sentence-internal temporal relations. In *Proceedings of the Human Language Technology Conference of the North American Chapter of the Association for Computational Linguistics: HLT-NAACL 2004*, pages 153–160, Boston, Massachusetts, USA. Association for Computational Linguistics.

Lee, A., Prasad, R., Joshi, A., Dinesh, N., and Webber, B. (2006). Complexity of dependencies in discourse: Are dependencies in discourse more complex than in syntax. In *Proceedings of the 5th International Workshop on Treebanks and Linguistic Theories.*

Lee, A., Prasad, R., Webber, B., and Joshi, A. K. (2016). Annotating discourse relations with the PDTB annotator. In *Proceedings of COLING 2016, the 26th International Conference on Computational Linguistics: System Demonstrations*, pages 121–125, Osaka, Japan.

Li, Y., Feng, W., Sun, J., Kong, F., and Zhou, G. (2014). Building Chinese discourse corpus with connective-driven dependency tree structure. In *Proceedings of the 2014 Conference on Empirical Methods in Natural Language Processing (EMNLP)*, pages 2105–2114, Doha, Qatar. Association for Computational Linguistics.

Li, Z., Zhao, H., Pang, C., Wang, L., and Wang, H. (2016). A constituent syntactic parse tree based discourse parser. In *Proceedings of the 20th Conference on Computational Natural Language Learning: Shared Task (CoNLL Shared Task 2016)*, pages 60–64, Berlin, Germany. Association for Computational Linguistics.

Lin, Z., Kan, M.-Y., and Ng, H. T. (2009). Recognizing implicit discourse relations in the Penn Discourse Treebank. In *Proceedings of the 2009 Conference on Empirical Methods in Natural Language Processing*, pages 343–351, Singapore. Association for Computational Linguistics.

Lin, Z., Ng, H. T., and Kan, M.-Y. (2014). A PDTB-Styled End-to-End Discourse Parser. *Natural Language Engineering*, 20:151–184.

Malmi, E., Pighin, D., Krause, S., and Kozhevnikov, M. (2018). Automatic prediction of discourse connectives. In *Proceedings of the 11th International Conference on Language Resources and Evaluation (LREC'18)*, Miyazaki, Japan. European Language Resources Association (ELRA).

Mann, W., Matthiessen, C., and Thompson, S. (1989). Rhetorical structure theory and text analysis. *Discourse Description: Diverse Linguistic Analyses of a Fund Raising Text*, page 66.

Mann, W. and Thompson, S. (1988). Rhetorical Structure Theory: Towards a functional theory of text organization. *TEXT*, 8:243–281.

Marcu, D. (2000). The rhetorical parsing of unrestricted texts: A surface-based approach. *Computational Linguistics*, 26(3):395–448.

Marcu, D. and Echihabi, A. (2002). An unsupervised approach to recognizing discourse relations. In *Proceedings of the 40th Annual Meeting of the Association for Computational Linguistics*, pages 368–375, Philadelphia, Pennsylvania, USA. Association for Computational Linguistics.

Marcus, M. P., Santorini, B., and Marcinkiewicz, M. A. (1993). Building a large annotated corpus of English: The Penn Treebank. *Computational Linguistics*, 19(2):313–330.

Maschler, Y. (2002). The role of discourse markers in the construction of multivocality in israeli hebrew talk in interaction. *Research on Language and Social Interaction*, 35(1):1–38.

Mendes, A. and Lejeune, P. (2016). LDM-PT. A Portuguese Lexicon of Discourse Markers. In *Conference Handbook of TextLink – Structuring Discourse in Multilingual Europe Second Action Conference*, pages 89–92, Budapest, Hungary.

Meyer, T. and Popescu-Belis, A. (2012). Using Sense-Labeled Discourse Connectives for Statistical Machine Translation. In *Proceedings of the Joint Workshop on Exploiting Synergies between Information Retrieval and Machine Translation (ESIRMT) and Hybrid Approaches to Machine Translation (HyTra)*, EACL 2012, page 129–138, USA. Association for Computational Linguistics.

Meyer, T., Popescu-Belis, A., Hajlaoui, N., and Gesmundo, A. (2012). Machine translation of labeled discourse connectives. In *Proceedings of the 10th Biennial Conference of the Association for Machine Translation in the Americas (AMTA)*.

Mihaylov, T. and Frank, A. (2016). Discourse relation sense classification using cross-argument semantic similarity based on word embeddings. In *Proceedings of the 20th Conference on Computational Natural Language Learning: Shared Task (CoNLL Shared Task 2016)*, pages 100–107, Berlin, Germany. Association for Computational Linguistics.

Mikolov, T., Sutskever, I., Chen, K., Corrado, G. S., and Dean, J. (2013). Distributed representations of words and phrases and their compositionality. In Burges, C. J. C., Bottou, L., Welling, M., Ghahramani, Z., and Weinberger, K. Q., editors, *Advances in Neural Information Processing Systems 26*, pages 3111–3119. Curran Associates, Inc.

Mírovský, J., Jínová, P., Rysová, M., and Poláková, L. (2016). Designing CzeDLex – a lexicon of Czech discourse connectives. In *Proceedings of the 30th Pacific Asia Conference on Language, Information and Computation: Posters*, pages 449–457, Seoul, South Korea.

Mulder, G. (2008). *Understanding Causal Coherence Relations*. PhD thesis, Utrecht University.

Nayak, S., Ramesh, R., and Shah, S. R. (2013). A study of multilabel text classification and the effect of label hierarchy.

Nivre, J., Abrams, M., Agić, Ž., Ahrenberg, L., Antonsen, L., Aplonova, K., Aranzabe, M. J., Arutie, G., Asahara, M., Ateyah, L., Attia, M., Atutxa, A., Augustinus, L., Badmaeva, E., Ballesteros, M., Banerjee, E., Bank, S., Barbu Mititelu, V., Basmov, V., Bauer, J., Bellato, S., Bengoetxea, K., Berzak, Y., Bhat, I. A., Bhat, R. A., Biagetti, E., Bick, E., Blokland, R., Bobicev, V., Börstell, C., Bosco, C., Bouma, G., Bowman, S., Boyd, A., Burchardt, A., Candito, M., Caron, B., Caron, G., Cebiroğlu Eryiğit, G., Cecchini, F. M., Celano, G. G. A., Čéplö, S., Cetin, S., Chalub, F., Choi, J., Cho, Y., Chun, J., Cinková, S., Collomb, A., Çöltekin, Ç., Connor, M., Courtin, M., Davidson, E., de Marneffe, M.-C., de Paiva, V., Diaz de Ilarraza, A., Dickerson, C., Dirix, P., Dobrovoljc, K., Dozat, T., Droganova, K., Dwivedi, P., Eli, M., Elkahky, A., Ephrem, B., Erjavec, T., Etienne, A., Farkas, R., Fernandez Alcalde, H., Foster, J., Freitas, C., Gajdošová, K., Galbraith, D., Garcia, M., Gärdenfors, M., Garza, S., Gerdes, K., Ginter, F., Goenaga, I., Gojenola, K., Gökırmak, M., Goldberg, Y., Gómez Guinovart, X., Gonzáles Saavedra, B., Grioni, M., Grūzītis, N., Guillaume, B., Guillot-Barbance, C., Habash, N., Hajič, J., Hajič jr., J., Hà Mỹ, L., Han, N.-R., Harris, K., Haug, D., Hladká, B.,

Hlaváčová, J., Hociung, F., Hohle, P., Hwang, J., Ion, R., Irimia, E., Ishola, Ọ., Jelínek, T., Johannsen, A., Jørgensen, F., Kaşıkara, H., Kahane, S., Kanayama, H., Kanerva, J., Katz, B., Kayadelen, T., Kenney, J., Kettnerová, V., Kirchner, J., Kopacewicz, K., Kotsyba, N., Krek, S., Kwak, S., Laippala, V., Lambertino, L., Lam, L., Lando, T., Larasati, S. D., Lavrentiev, A., Lee, J., Lê Hồng, P., Lenci, A., Lertpradit, S., Leung, H., Li, C. Y., Li, J., Li, K., Lim, K., Ljubešić, N., Loginova, O., Lyashevskaya, O., Lynn, T., Macketanz, V., Makazhanov, A., Mandl, M., Manning, C., Manurung, R., Mărănduc, C., Mareček, D., Marheinecke, K., Martínez Alonso, H., Martins, A., Mašek, J., Matsumoto, Y., McDonald, R., Mendonça, G., Miekka, N., Misirpashayeva, M., Missilä, A., Mititelu, C., Miyao, Y., Montemagni, S., More, A., Moreno Romero, L., Mori, K. S., Mori, S., Mortensen, B., Moskalevskyi, B., Muischnek, K., Murawaki, Y., Müürisep, K., Nainwani, P., Navarro Horñiacek, J. I., Nedoluzhko, A., Nešpore-Bērzkalne, G., Nguyễn Thị, L., Nguyễn Thị Minh, H., Nikolaev, V., Nitisaroj, R., Nurmi, H., Ojala, S., Olúòkun, A., Omura, M., Osenova, P., Östling, R., Øvrelid, L., Partanen, N., Pascual, E., Passarotti, M., Patejuk, A., Paulino-Passos, G., Peng, S., Perez, C.-A., Perrier, G., Petrov, S., Piitulainen, J., Pitler, E., Plank, B., Poibeau, T., Popel, M., Pretkalniņa, L., Prévost, S., Prokopidis, P., Przepiórkowski, A., Puolakainen, T., Pyysalo, S., Rääbis, A., Rademaker, A., Ramasamy, L., Rama, T., Ramisch, C., Ravishankar, V., Real, L., Reddy, S., Rehm, G., Rießler, M., Rinaldi, L., Rituma, L., Rocha, L., Romanenko, M., Rosa, R., Rovati, D., Roșca, V., Rudina, O., Rueter, J., Sadde, S., Sagot, B., Saleh, S., Samardžić, T., Samson, S., Sanguinetti, M., Saulīte, B., Sawanakunanon, Y., Schneider, N., Schuster, S., Seddah, D., Seeker, W., Seraji, M., Shen, M., Shimada, A., Shohibussirri, M., Sichinava, D., Silveira, N., Simi, M., Simionescu, R., Simkó, K., Šimková, M., Simov, K., Smith, A., Soares-Bastos, I., Spadine, C., Stella, A., Straka, M., Strnadová, J., Suhr, A., Sulubacak, U., Szántó, Z., Taji, D., Takahashi, Y., Tanaka, T., Tellier, I., Trosterud, T., Trukhina, A., Tsarfaty, R., Tyers, F., Uematsu, S., Urešová, Z., Uria, L., Uszkoreit, H., Vajjala, S., van Niekerk, D., van Noord, G., Varga, V., Villemonte de la Clergerie, E., Vincze, V., Wallin, L., Wang, J. X., Washington, J. N., Williams, S., Wirén, M., Woldemariam, T., Wong, T.-s., Yan, C., Yavrumyan, M. M., Yu, Z., Žabokrtský, Z., Zeldes,

A., Zeman, D., Zhang, M., and Zhu, H. (2018). Universal dependencies 2.3. LINDAT/CLARIN digital library at the Institute of Formal and Applied Linguistics (ÚFAL), Faculty of Mathematics and Physics, Charles University.

Nothman, J., Ringland, N., Radford, W., Murphy, T., and Curran, J. R. (2013). Learning Multilingual Named Entity Recognition from Wikipedia. *Artificial Intelligence*, 194:151–175.

Oepen, S., Read, J., Scheffler, T., Sidarenka, U., Stede, M., Velldal, E., and Øvrelid, L. (2016). OPT: Oslo–Potsdam–Teesside—Pipelining Rules, Rankers, and Classifier Ensembles for Shallow Discourse Parsing. In *Proceedings of the 20th Conference on Computational Natural Language Learning: Shared Task (CoNLL Shared Task 2016)*, pages 20–26, Berlin.

Ostendorff, M., Bourgonje, P., Berger, M., Moreno-Schneider, J., and Rehm, G. (2019). Enriching BERT with Knowledge Graph Embeddings for Document Classification. In Remus, S., Aly, R., and Biemann, C., editors, *Proceedings of the GermEval Workshop 2019 – Shared Task on the Hierarchical Classification of Blurbs*, Erlangen, Germany.

Pacheco, M. L., Lee, I.-T., Zhang, X., Zehady, A. K., Daga, P., Jin, D., Parolia, A., and Goldwasser, D. (2016). Adapting event embedding for implicit discourse relation recognition. In *Proceedings of the 20th Conference on Computational Natural Language Learning: Shared Task (CoNLL Shared Task 2016)*, pages 136–142, Berlin, Germany. Association for Computational Linguistics.

Pander Maat, H. (2002). *Tekstanalyse: Wat teksten tot teksten maakt.* Coutinho, Bussum.

Pasch, R., Brauße, U., Breindl, E., and Waßner, U. H. (2003). *Handbuch der deutschen Konnektoren.* Walter de Gruyter, Berlin/New York.

Pedregosa, F., Varoquaux, G., Gramfort, A., Michel, V., Thirion, B., Grisel, O., Blondel, M., Prettenhofer, P., Weiss, R., Dubourg, V., Vanderplas, J., Passos, A., Cournapeau, D., Brucher, M., Perrot, M., and Duchesnay, E. (2011). Scikit-learn: Machine Learning in Python. *Journal of Machine Learning Research*, 12:2825–2830.

Péry-Woodley, M.-P., S.D., A., Ho-Dac, L.-M., and Asher, N. (2011). Le corpus ANNODIS, un corpus enrichi d'annotations discursives. *TAL*, 52(3):71–101.

Peters, M., Neumann, M., Iyyer, M., Gardner, M., Clark, C., Lee, K., and Zettlemoyer, L. (2018). Deep contextualized word representations. In *Proceedings of the 2018 Conference of the North American Chapter of the Association for Computational Linguistics: Human Language Technologies, Volume 1 (Long Papers)*, pages 2227–2237, New Orleans, Louisiana. Association for Computational Linguistics.

Pitler, E., Louis, A., and Nenkova, A. (2009). Automatic sense prediction for implicit discourse relations in text. In *Proceedings of the Joint Conference of the 47th Annual Meeting of the ACL and the 4th International Joint Conference on Natural Language Processing of the AFNLP*, pages 683–691, Suntec, Singapore. Association for Computational Linguistics.

Pitler, E. and Nenkova, A. (2009). Using syntax to disambiguate explicit discourse connectives in text. In *Proceedings of the ACL-IJCNLP 2009 Conference Short Papers*, pages 13–16, Suntec, Singapore. Association for Computational Linguistics.

Prasad, R., Dinesh, N., Lee, A., Joshi, A., and Webber, B. (2006a). Annotating attribution in the penn discourse treebank. In *Proceedings of the Workshop on Sentiment and Subjectivity in Text*, SST '06, page 31–38, USA. Association for Computational Linguistics.

Prasad, R., Dinesh, N., Lee, A., Miltsakaki, E., Robaldo, L., Joshi, A., and Webber, B. (2008). The Penn discourse TreeBank 2.0. In *Proceedings of the Sixth International Conference on Language Resources and Evaluation (LREC'08)*, pages 2961–2968, Marrakech, Morocco. European Language Resources Association (ELRA).

Prasad, R., Miltsakaki, E., Dinesh, N., Lee, A., and Joshi, A. (2007). The Penn Discourse Treebank 2.0 Annotation Manual.

Prasad, R., Miltsakaki, E., Dinesh, N., Lee, A., Joshi, A., and Webber, B. (2006b). The Penn Discourse Treebank 1.0 annotation manual.

Prasad, R., Webber, B., Lee, A., and Joshi, A. (2019). Penn Discourse Treebank Version 3.0, LDC2019T05.

Qin, L., Zhang, Z., and Zhao, H. (2016). Shallow discourse parsing using convolutional neural network. In *Proceedings of the 20th Conference on Computational Natural Language Learning: Shared Task (CoNLL Shared Task 2016)*, pages 70–77, Berlin, Germany. Association for Computational Linguistics.

Radford, A., Wu, J., Child, R., Luan, D., Amodei, D., and Sutskever, I. (2019). Language models are unsupervised multitask learners.

Rafferty, A. N. and Manning, C. D. (2008). Parsing Three German Treebanks: Lexicalized and Unlexicalized Baselines. In *Proceedings of the Workshop on Parsing German*, PaGe '08, pages 40–46. Association for Computational Linguistics.

Rajpurkar, P., Jia, R., and Liang, P. (2018). Know what you don't know: Unanswerable questions for SQuAD. In *Proceedings of the 56th Annual Meeting of the Association for Computational Linguistics (Volume 2: Short Papers)*, pages 784–789, Melbourne, Australia. Association for Computational Linguistics.

Redeker, G. (1991). Linguistic markers of discourse structure. *Linguistics*, 26:1139–1172.

Redeker, G., Berzlánovich, I., van der Vliet, N., Bouma, G., and Egg, M. (2012). Multi-layer discourse annotation of a dutch text corpus. In Chair), N. C. C., Choukri, K., Declerck, T., Doğan, M. U., Maegaard, B., Mariani, J., Moreno, A., Odijk, J., and Piperidis, S., editors, *Proceedings of the Eight International Conference on Language Resources and Evaluation (LREC'12)*, Istanbul, Turkey. European Language Resources Association (ELRA).

Reese, B., Hunter, J., Asher, N., Denis, P., and Baldridge, J. (2007). Reference Manual for the Analysis and Annotation of Rhetorical Structure (Version 1.0).

Rösner, D. and Stede, M. (1992). Customizing rst for the automatic production of technical manuals. In Dale, R., Hovy, E., Rösner, D., and Stock, O., editors, *Aspects of Automated Natural Language Generation*, pages 199–214, Berlin, Heidelberg. Springer Berlin Heidelberg.

Roze, C., Danlos, L., and Muller, P. (2012). LEXCONN: A French lexicon of discourse connectives. *Discours. Revue de linguistique, psycholinguistique et informatique*, 10.

Rutherford, A., Demberg, V., and Xue, N. (2017). A systematic study of neural discourse models for implicit discourse relation. In *Proceedings of the 15th Conference of the European Chapter of the Association for Computational Linguistics: Volume 1, Long Papers*, pages 281–291, Valencia, Spain. Association for Computational Linguistics.

Rysová, M., Jínová, P., Mírovský, J., Hajičová, E., Nedoluzhko, A., Ocelák, R., Pergler, J., Poláková, L., Zdeňková, J., Scheller, V., and Zikánová, Š. (2016). Prague discourse treebank 2.0.

Sabatini-Coletti (2005). *Dizionario della lingua italiana*. Rizzoli

Larousse.

Sanders, T. and Noordman, L. (2000). The role of coherence relations and their linguistic markers in text processing. *Discourse Processes*, 29(1):37–60.

Sanders, T. J., Demberg, V., Hoek, J., Scholman, M. C., Asr, F. T., Zufferey, S., and Evers-Vermeul, J. (2018). Unifying dimensions in coherence relations: How various annotation frameworks are related. *Corpus Linguistics and Linguistic Theory*.

Sanders, T. J., Spooren, W. P., and Noordman, L. G. (1992). Toward a taxonomy of coherence relations. *Discourse Processes*, 15(1):1–35.

Scheffler, T. and Stede, M. (2016). Adding Semantic Relations to a Large-Coverage Connective Lexicon of German. In et al., N. C., editor, *Proceedings of the 10th International Conference on Language Resources and Evaluation (LREC'16)*, pages 1008–1013, Portorož, Slovenia. European Language Resources Association (ELRA).

Schiffrin, D. (1987). *Discourse Markers*. Studies in Interactional Sociolinguistics. Cambridge University Press.

Shi, W. and Demberg, V. (2019). Next sentence prediction helps implicit discourse relation classification within and across domains. In *Proceedings of the 2019 Conference on Empirical Methods in Natural Language Processing and the 9th International Joint Conference on Natural Language Processing (EMNLP-IJCNLP)*, pages 5790–5796, Hong Kong, China. Association for Computational Linguistics.

Sluyter-Gäthje, H., Bourgonje, P., and Stede, M. (2020). Shallow discourse parsing for under-resourced languages: Combining machine translation and annotation projection. In *Proceedings of the 12th Language Resources and Evaluation Conference (LREC'20)*, pages 1044–1050, Marseille, France. European Language Resources Association (ELRA).

Sporleder, C. and Lascarides, A. (2005). Exploiting linguistic cues to classify rhetorical relations. In *Proceedings of Recent Advances in Natural Language Processing (RANLP-05)*, pages 532–539. Association for Computational Linguistics - Bulgaria.

Sporleder, C. and Lascarides, A. (2008). Using automatically labelled examples to classify rhetorical relations: An assessment. *Natural Language Engineering*, 14(3):369–416.

Stede, M. (2002). DiMLex: A Lexical Approach to Discourse Markers. In *Exploring the Lexicon - Theory and Computation*. Edizioni dell'Orso, Alessandria.

Stede, M. (2004). The Potsdam Commentary Corpus. In *Proceedings of the 2004 ACL Workshop on Discourse Annotation*, pages 96–102. Association for Computational Linguistics.

Stede, M., editor (2015). *Handbuch Textannotation*. Potsdamer Kommentarkorpus 2.0. Universitätsverlag Potsdam.

Stede, M. and Heintze, S. (2004). Machine-assisted rhetorical structure annotation. In *COLING 2004: Proceedings of the 20th International Conference on Computational Linguistics*, pages 425–431, Geneva, Switzerland. COLING.

Stede, M. and Neumann, A. (2014). Potsdam commentary corpus 2.0: Annotation for discourse research. In *Proceedings of the Ninth International Conference on Language Resources and Evaluation (LREC'14)*, pages 925–929, Reykjavik, Iceland. European Language Resources Association (ELRA).

Stede, M., Scheffler, T., and Mendes, A. (2019). Connective-lex: A web-based multilingual lexical resource for connectives. *Discours. Revue de linguistique, psycholinguistique et informatique*.

Stede, M. and Umbach, C. (1998). DiMLex: A lexicon of discourse markers for text generation and understanding. In *36th Annual Meeting of the Association for Computational Linguistics and 17th International Conference on Computational Linguistics, Volume 2*, pages 1238–1242, Montreal, Quebec, Canada. Association for Computational Linguistics.

Stepanov, E. and Riccardi, G. (2016). UniTN end-to-end discourse parser for CoNLL 2016 shared task. In *Proceedings of the 20th Conference on Computational Natural Language Learning: Shared Task (CoNLL Shared Task 2016)*, pages 85–91, Berlin, Germany. Association for Computational Linguistics.

Telljohann, H., Hinrichs, E. W., Kübler, S., Zinsmeister, H., and Beck, K. (2012). *Stylebook for the Tübingen Treebank of Written German (TüBa-D/Z)*. Seminar für Sprachwissenschaft, Wilhelmstr. 19, D-72074 Tübingen.

Tiedemann, J. (2012). Parallel data, tools and interfaces in opus. In Calzolari, N., Choukri, K., Declerck, T., Doğan, M. U., Maegaard, B., Mariani, J., Moreno, A., Odijk, J., and Piperidis., S., editors, *Proceedings of the Eight International Conference on Language Resources and Evaluation (LREC'12)*, pages 2214–2218, Istanbul, Turkey. European Language Resources Association (ELRA).

Toldova, S., Pisarevskaya, D., Ananyeva, M., Kobozeva, M., Nasedkin, A., Nikiforova, S., Pavlova, I., and Shelepov, A. (2017). Rhetorical relations markers in Russian RST Treebank. In *Proceedings of the 6th Workshop on Recent Advances in RST and Related Formalisms*, pages 29–33. Association for Computational Linguistics.

Van Noord, G. (2006). At Last Parsing Is Now Operational. In *TALN06. Verbum Ex Machina. Actes de la 13e conference sur le traitement automatique des langues naturelles.*, pages 20–42, Leuven. Leuven University Press.

Van Wijk, C. and Kempen, G. (1980). Funktiewoorden: Een inventarisatie voor het Nederlands (An inventory of Dutch function words). *ITL-International Journal of Applied Linguistics*, 47(1):53–68.

Versley, Y. (2010). Discovery of ambiguous and unambiguous discourse connectives via annotation projection. In Ahrenberg, L., Tiedemann, J., and Volk, M., editors, *Proceedings of Workshop on Annotation and Exploitation of Parallel Corpora (AEPC)*, pages 83–92. Northern European Association for Language Technology (NEALT).

Versley, Y. and Gastel, A. (2013). Linguistic tests for discourse relations in the TüBa-D/Z corpus of written German. *Dialogue and Discourse*, 4(2):142–173.

Wang, F., Wu, Y., and Qiu, L. (2012). Exploiting discourse relations for sentiment analysis. In *Proceedings of COLING 2012: Posters*, pages 1311–1320, Mumbai, India. The COLING 2012 Organizing Committee.

Wang, J. and Lan, M. (2015). A Refined End-to-End Discourse Parser. In *Proceedings of the 19th Conference on Computational Natural Language Learning: Shared Task (CoNLL Shared Task 2015)*, pages 17–24. Association for Computational Linguistics.

Wang, J. and Lan, M. (2016). Two end-to-end shallow discourse parsers for English and Chinese in CoNLL-2016 shared task. In *Proceedings of the 20th Conference on Computational Natural Language Learning: Shared Task (CoNLL Shared Task 2016)*, pages 33–40, Berlin, Germany. Association for Computational Linguistics.

Webber, B., Prasad, R., Lee, A., and Joshi, A. (2019). The Penn Discourse Treebank 3.0 Annotation Manual.

Wellner, B. and Pustejovsky, J. (2007). Automatically identifying the arguments of discourse connectives. In *Proceedings of the 2007 Joint Conference on Empirical Methods in Natural Language Processing and Computational Natural Language Learning (EMNLP-CoNLL)*, pages 92–101, Prague, Czech Republic. Association for Computational Linguistics.

Xue, N., Ng, H. T., Pradhan, S., Prasad, R., Bryant, C., and Rutherford, A. (2015). The CoNLL-2015 Shared Task on Shallow Discourse Parsing. In *Proceedings of the 19th Conference on Computational Natural Language Learning: Shared Task (CoNLL Shared Task 2015)*, pages 1–16. Association for Computational Linguistics.

Xue, N., Ng, H. T., Pradhan, S., Rutherford, A., Webber, B., Wang, C., and Wang, H. (2016). CoNLL 2016 shared task on multilingual shallow discourse parsing. In *Proceedings of the 20th Conference on Computational Natural Language Learning: Shared Task (CoNLL Shared Task 2016)*, pages 1–19, Berlin, Germany. Association for Computational Linguistics.

Zeldes, A. (2017). The GUM corpus: creating multilayer resources in the classroom. *Language Resources and Evaluation*, 51(3):581–612.

Zeldes, A., Das, D., Maziero, E. G., Antonio, J., and Iruskieta, M. (2019). The DISRPT 2019 shared task on elementary discourse unit segmentation and connective detection. In *Proceedings of the Workshop on Discourse Relation Parsing and Treebanking 2019*, pages 97–104, Minneapolis, MN. Association for Computational Linguistics.

Zellers, R., Bisk, Y., Schwartz, R., and Choi, Y. (2018). SWAG: A large-scale adversarial dataset for grounded commonsense inference. In *Proceedings of the 2018 Conference on Empirical Methods in Natural Language Processing*, pages 93–104, Brussels, Belgium. Association for Computational Linguistics.

Zeyrek, D., Demirsahin, I., Sevdik-Calli, A. B., Balaban, H. Ö., Yalcinkaya, I., and Turan, U. D. (2010). The annotation scheme of the turkish discourse bank and an evaluation of inconsistent annotations. In *Proceedings of the Fourth Linguistic Annotation Workshop, LAW 2010*, pages 282–289.

Zeyrek, D. and Kurfalı, M. (2017). TDB 1.1: Extensions on Turkish discourse bank. In *Proceedings of the 11th Linguistic Annotation Workshop*, pages 76–81, Valencia, Spain. Association for Computational Linguistics.

Zeyrek, D., Mendes, A., Grishina, Y., Kurfalı, M., Gibbon, S., and Ogrodniczuk, M. (2020). TED Multilingual Discourse Bank (TED-MDB): a parallel corpus annotated in the PDTB style. *Language Resources and Evaluation*, 54:587–613.

Zhou, Y. and Xue, N. (2015). The Chinese Discourse TreeBank: A Chinese Corpus Annotated with Discourse Relations. *Language Resources and Evaluation*, 49(2):397–431.

9 781643 681924